Hemingway and
the Mechanism of Fame

This caricature accompanied the editorial ". . . and New Champion" in *Collier's* 126 (18 November 1950): 8G. The Al Hirschfeld drawing was probably inspired by John O'Hara's identification of Ernest Hemingway as "the outstanding author since the death of Shakespeare" in the *New York Times Book Review,* 10 September 1950, 1, 30–31. © Al Hirschfeld / Margo Feiden Galleries Ltd., New York. www.alhirschfeld.com

Hemingway and the Mechanism of Fame

STATEMENTS, PUBLIC LETTERS, INTRODUCTIONS, FOREWORDS, PREFACES, BLURBS, REVIEWS, AND ENDORSEMENTS

EDITED BY Matthew J. Bruccoli

with Judith S. Baughman

UNIVERSITY OF SOUTH CAROLINA PRESS

© 2006 University of South Carolina

Published by the University of South Carolina Press
Columbia, South Carolina 29208

www.sc.edu/uscpress

Manufactured in the United States of America

15 14 13 12 11 10 09 08 07 06   10 9 8 7 6 5 4 3 2 1

Library of Congress Cataloging-in-Publication Data

Hemingway, Ernest, 1899–1961.
 Hemingway and the mechanism of fame : statements, public letters, introductions, forewords, prefaces, blurbs, reviews, and endorsements / edited by Matthew J. Bruccoli with Judith S. Baughman.
  p. cm.
 Includes bibliographical references (p.   ) and index.
 ISBN 1-57003-599-7 (alk. paper)
 1. Authors and readers—United States—History—20th century—Sources. I. Bruccoli, Matthew Joseph, 1931– II. Baughman, Judith. III. Title.
 PS3515.E37A6 2005
 813'.52—dc22

                                                    2005015890

FOR JOHN UNRUE

Contents

Illustrations and Facsimiles

Acknowledgments

My approach to Hemingway's reputation and influence builds on John Raeburn's admirable *Fame Became of Him: Hemingway as Public Writer* (Bloomington: Indiana University Press, 1984). I am also indebted to colleagues at the Thomas Cooper Library, University of South Carolina: Jo Cottingham, Interlibrary Loan Department, found elusive Hemingway material; and Elizabeth Sudduth, Rare Books and Special Collections, provided access to the Speiser and Easterling-Hallman Foundation Collection of Ernest Hemingway. Jill Jividen ably assisted with research and proofing. Lydia Zelaya, Permission Department, Simon & Schuster, always aids my projects.

All texts and illustrations are located, with the exception of readily available mass-circulation magazines and newspapers.

This book began as a project with Vernon Sternberg. I stopped work on it when Vern died in 1979. Many things ended with him. The volume was resuscitated in 2003.

M.J.B.

Introduction

I

When Ernest Hemingway published his disappointing novel *Across the River and into the Trees* in 1950, John O'Hara's article in the *New York Times Book Review* identified him as "The most important author living today, the outstanding author since the death of Shakespeare."* This proclamation generated incredulity and ridicule; but it was probably accurate if "American" is inserted before "author."

Hemingway combined nonliterary fame with literary stature. Few American writers have had both: Hemingway, Mark Twain, and F. Scott Fitzgerald—who achieved it posthumously. One gauge of an American writer's stature at his death is the length and placement of the *New York Times* obituary. On 3 July 1961 the *Times* accorded Hemingway three columns with a two-column photo above the fold on the front page, five full columns on page 6, an assessment by *Times* book reviewer Charles Poore, and tributes by seventeen literary figures—including John Dos Passos, Robert Frost, and William Faulkner, who provided a Faulknerian statement that was scrambled by the compositors:

> One of the bravest and best, the strictest in principles, the severest of craftsmen, undeviating in his dedication to the believable moment the antics craft: which is to arrest for a of human beings involved in the comedy and tragedy of being alive. To the few who knew him well he was almost as good a man as the books he wrote. He is not dead. Generations not yet born of young men and women who want to write will refute that word as applied to him.

At the time of Hemingway's death literary historian Malcolm Cowley tried to convey a sense of the force of his character:

> If Hemingway had appeared on a South Sea island two centuries ago, he would have been made a chief, his toenail parings would have been

* *New York Times Book Review,* 10 September 1950, 1, 30–31.

burned to protect them from commoners, and after his death he would have been deified.*

Hemingway had enjoyed the experience of reading his obituaries while he was alive, after the false reports of his death in 1954. The news of the African plane crash and his survival made the *Times* and *New York Herald Tribune* front pages for two days. The *Trib* also provided an editorial celebrating his endurance: "It is, somehow, characteristic of Ernest Hemingway that he should walk away from two plane crashes in the heart of Africa. Death has been his familiar companion for many years—an association freely accepted, even courted by the author, as if the dark shadow by his side threw his own abounding vitality into higher relief."†

Hemingway was easily the most famous writer in the world at the time of his suicide. His reputation and stature have fluctuated during the forty years since his death, but there has been no major reappraisal. Hemingway's work has withstood the depredations of political correctness, feminism, deconstruction, and postmodernism. He remains the most recognizable American writer. He photographed well, and he provided a ready subject for caricatures. People who have never read his books—or any books—identify his face as that of "some kind of writer." Hemingway was famous for being famous. Archibald MacLeish, his on-and-off friend, wrote of him:

> And what became of him? Fame became of him.
>   Veteran out of the wars before he was twenty:
>   Famous at twenty-five: thirty a master——§

This tribute characteristically exaggerates Hemingway's war record: he was a World War I veteran by courtesy, having been wounded distributing chocolate and tobacco while serving with the Red Cross.

Hemingway's extra-literary activities made the practice of authorship respectable to civilians who were suspicious of writing as an occupation for grown men. At the same time he may have damaged the profession of authorship by providing readers with a distorted model for how writers were supposed to live and work: writers who didn't emulate Hemingway were regarded as minor figures or hobbyists or sissies. Many would-be writers wanted to be writers so that they could live like Hemingway.

Hemingway's fame was not a spontaneous response to his books. He deliberately cultivated and manipulated his public images. Ernest Hemingway's

---

* "One Man's Hemingway," *New York Herald Tribune Book Review,* 9 July 1961, 3, 15.
† *Herald Tribune,* 26 January 1954, 16.
§ Archibald MacLeish, *Years of the Dog, Actfive and Other Poems* (New York: Random House, 1948), 53.

best-invented fictional character was Ernest Hemingway—really a cluster of characters: hunter, fisherman, soldier, aesthetician, patriot, military strategist, yachtsman, drinker, womanizer, gourmet, sportsman, philosopher, naturalist, intellectual, anti-intellectual, traveler, war correspondent, boxer, big-game hunter—and author. In each of these roles he projected the authority of the professional: the man who knows the right way to do it and can do it correctly; the man who knows the true gen and the inside dope; the writer with the "built-in, shock-proof, shit detector."* More than any other American writer, he became identified with his characters. His fiction was read as autobiography: Jake Barnes, Frederic Henry, and Robert Jordan were assumed to be Hemingway—or at least to have been based on him. He was not scrupulous about correcting the false connections between his life and his fiction—apart from denying that he had suffered Barnes's penile wound.

Although Hemingway complained about invasions of his privacy and interference with his working time, he was available to journalists and photographers. He pal-ed around with gossip columnists. The camera loved him: Hemingway with large dead animals, Hemingway with large fish, Hemingway with bullfighters, Hemingway with beautiful women, Hemingway in war, Hemingway in glamorous places, Hemingway with famous men. The extraordinary element of his self-generated celebrity is that everything he did apart from writing seemed to have something to do with literature. Other writers were rebuked for self-indulgence or irresponsibility—by critics and by Hemingway—when they left their desks; but it was somehow understood that Hemingway was fishing, hunting, boozing, wenching, and brawling for the eventual enrichment of American literature.

The *Pilar* provides a gauge of his incremental fame. Hemingway's fishing boat was thirty-eight feet long when he bought it in 1934; at the time of his death it had grown into a legendary vessel, along with the *Constitution,* the *Cutty Sark,* and the *Ile de France.*

He wrote forcefully and convincingly about the value of literature and the force of his commitment to it.

> A country, finally, erodes and the dust blows away, the people all die and none of them were of any importance permanently, except those who practiced the arts, and these now wish to cease their work because it is too lonely, too hard to do, and is not fashionable. A thousand years makes economics silly and a work of art endures forever, but it is very difficult to do and now it is not fashionable.†

* George Plimpton, "The Art of Fiction: Ernest Hemingway," *The Paris Review* 5 (Spring 1958): 60–89.
† Ernest Hemingway, *Green Hills of Africa* (New York: Scribners, 1935), 109.

Hemingway's testimonies about his dedication to his craft take the form of boasting. For him the profession of authorship was a blood competition. In 1949 he analyzed his achievements and ambitions for his publisher, Charles Scribner III:

Am a man without any ambition, except to be champion of the world, I wouldn't fight Dr. Tolstoi in a 20 round bout because I know he would knock my ears off. The Dr. had terrific wind and could go forever and then some. But I would take him on for six and he would never hit me and would knock the shit out of him and maybe knock him out. He is easy to hit. But boy how he can hit. If I can live to 60 I can beat him. (MAYBE)

For your information I started out trying to beat dead writers that I knew how good they were. (Excuse vernacular) I tried for Mr. Turgenieff first and it wasn't too hard. Tried for Mr. Maupassant (won't concede him the de) and it took four of the best stories to beat him. He's beaten and if he was around he would know it. Then I tried for another guy (am getting embarrassed or embare-assed now from bragging; or stateing) and I think I fought a draw with him. This other dead character.

Mr. Henry James I would just thumb him once the first time he grabbed and then hit him once where he had no balls and ask the referee to stop it.

There are some guys nobody could ever beat like Mr. Shakespeare (The Champion) and Mr. Anonymous. But would be glad any time, if in training, to go twenty with Mr. Cervantes in his own home town (Alcala de Henares) and beat the shit out of him. Although Mr. C. very smart and would be learning all the time and would probably beat you in a return match. The third fight people would pay to see. Plenty peoples.

But these Brooklyn jerks are so ignorant that they start off fighting Mr. Tolstoi. And they announce they have beaten him before the fight starts. They should be hung by the balls until dead for ignorance. I can write good and I would not get into the ring with Mr. T. over the long distance unless I and my family were not eating.

In the big book I hope to take Mr. Melville and Mr. Doestoevsky, they are coupled as a stable entry, and throw lots of mud in their faces because the track isn't fast. But you can only run so many of those kind of races. They take it out of you.

Know this sounds like bragging but Jeezoo Chrise you have to have confidence to be a champion and that is the only thing I ever wished to be.*

* 6 and 7 September 1949; *Selected Letters,* ed. Carlos Baker (New York: Scribners, 1981), 673.

Hemingway got away with his braggadocio because his readers wanted to believe him. Why they wanted to believe him is unclear.

II

Ernest Hemingway utilized the items assembled here to shape and maintain his fame between books. No matter what the ostensible subject was, all of the items are about himself. The totals are fifty-four statements and public letters; twenty introductions, forewords, and prefaces; twenty-nine blurbs, reviews, and endorsements. These categories overlap. Hemingway's life and career were driven by his need for self-dramatization. When he wasn't writing for publication, he compulsively dispatched hundreds—probably thousands—of letters shaping and augmenting the Hemingway legends.

This volume is restricted to items that Hemingway wrote for publication; printed excerpts from his correspondence are excluded unless it is clear that he intended them to be printed. Interviews are omitted as a category because they have already been collected in *Conversations with Ernest Hemingway* (Jackson: University Press of Mississippi, 1986); but Hemingway's published written responses to questions have been included. This collection is organized chronologically to provide a sense of Hemingway's evolving public persona. Make that personae. He was able to project the image that the time or occasion required. In the Twenties he was contemptuous of noble causes and patriotism; during the early Thirties he was apolitical; during the Spanish Civil War he was an anti-fascist activist; during World War II he was a patriot. These modulations did not hurt sales of his books. Eventually the bruiser became the sage who appeared on the cover of *Wisdom*.

Those seeking consistency in Hemingway's roles will find it most clearly in "The Man of Letters." When he discoursed on writing he did it with what Fitzgerald identified as "the authority of success."* His early detractors portrayed him as a "dumb ox"; but while they were writing term papers, Hemingway was taking tutorials with Ezra Pound, James Joyce, and Gertrude Stein. While they were editing their college literary magazines, he was editing the *transatlantic review* with Ford Madox Ford and being published by William Bird, Robert McAlmon, and Ezra Pound. Hemingway's comments on the craft and standards of literature document his wide reading, high requirements, literary intelligence, and contempt for critical fashions.

Hemingway's practice of literary criticism was always personal. It was also a form of vendetta. Thus his response to the death of Joseph Conrad provided an opportunity to denigrate T. S. Eliot: "If I knew that by grinding Mr. Eliot

---

* F. Scott Fitzgerald, *The Notebooks* (New York: Harcourt Brace Jovanovich/Bruccoli Clark, 1978), #1915.

into a fine dry powder and sprinkling that powder over Mr. Conrad's grave Mr. Conrad would shortly appear, looking very annoyed at the forced return and commence writing I would leave for London early tomorrow morning with a sausage grinder." That wisecrack does not disclose Eliot's literary capital crimes—which included being more admired than Hemingway in 1924—but it delivers the message that Hemingway was ready to kill for the sake of literature. Other long-term grudge fights were with Gertrude Stein, Waldo Frank, and, intermittently, William Faulkner—whose offenses included winning the Nobel Prize before Hemingway.

With the exception of the Stein feud, which she triggered by ridiculing him in *The Autobiography of Alice B. Toklas* (1933), Hemingway's feuds were one-sided. F. Scott Fitzgerald, who was the target of Hemingway's ridicule, alive and dead, observed in his *Notebooks* that "Ernest would always give a helping hand to a man on a ledge a little higher up."[*] Hemingway consistently extolled Tolstoy, Turgenev, Stendhal, Joyce, and Pound—none of whom constituted competition or made claims for his influence on Hemingway.[†]

Much of Hemingway's literary criticism consists of blurbs and reading lists. He did not write a book review after 1925. He maintained distrust and scorn for critics—especially those of the academic persuasion. In *Green Hills of Africa* (1935) he identified critics as "All angleworms in a bottle, trying to derive knowledge and nourishment from their own contact and from the bottle."[‡] Yet he forcefully asserted that the profession of literature was a fit endeavor for serious men—and few women. His standards were masculine: good writers had balls; bad writers were sissy-boys; his detractors were fairies, lesbians, or virgins of both sexes.

The range of books and authors endorsed by Hemingway is characteristic of his stance as an anti-intellectual intellectual: from high culture to sportswriting, from Ezra Pound and Archibald MacLeish to Jimmy Cannon and Red Smith. He was not a promiscuous blurber. Some of his endorsements—for MacLeish, Pound, Josephine Herbst, John Herrmann, and George Plimpton—were in part acts of friendship; others were apparently unsolicited responses to novels he admired: W. C. Heinz's *The Professional*, C. S. Forester's *Beat to Quarters*, Nelson Algren's *The Man with the Golden Arm*.

The element Hemingway most admired in fiction was the accuracy that resulted from the writer's knowledge of the way it was, based on observation and experience, accurately reported. The word *truly* echoes throughout his nonfiction and fiction. He subscribed to Maxwell Perkins's dictum that "the

---

[*] Ibid., # 1819.
[†] A monograph on the Hemingway/Pound connection is needed.
[‡] Hemingway, *Green Hills of Africa,* 21.

utterly real thing in writing is the only thing that counts."* The getting-it-right test permeates his own work, as well as his judgments on other authors. Worthless books were written by fakers who didn't know what they were writing about.

III

Hemingway's rejection of political causes and writers who professed them was manifest before the Spanish Civil War. During the early Thirties when leftist orthodoxy was a requirement for literary merit and intellectual respectability, Hemingway sneered at the political converts and conformists. He insisted that political doctrines had nothing to do with enduring literature. *To Have and Have Not* (1937) ridicules the proletarian school of fiction and its practitioners, but most of the fellow-travelers didn't get it. They wanted to read it as a Steinbeckian sermon and claim Hemingway as a fellow fellow-traveler. During the Spanish Civil War he wrote pro-Loyalist statements, public letters, and introductory material for publications affiliated with the Communists. Josephine Herbst, who was in Spain with Hemingway, diagnosed the war's pull on him: "He wanted to be the war writer of his age and he knew it and went toward it."† The party-liners fancied that they had a proselyte; but Hemingway was a non-communist anti-fascist. He did not sell out to the leftist critical establishment to refurbish his literary position, which had been bruised by denunciations of *Death in the Afternoon* (1932) and *Green Hills of Africa* (1935) as decadent and irrelevant in the Depression.

Hemingway maintained his complex honesty and suspicion of organizations. He divided the world into two categories: Insiders (us) and Outsiders (them). His writings provided readers with membership in the Insiders Club. As the ultimate Insider he was determined to obtain the real dope about the Spanish Civil War and use it. But Hemingway's emotional involvement with the international brigades and their volunteers penetrated his writings during the war. The combination of war and adultery in Madrid influenced his didactic play *The Fifth Column* (1938). But the zealots who had celebrated his Loyalist activities in Spain were outraged by *For Whom the Bell Tolls* (1940). Alvah Bessie's attack in *The Heart of Spain* (published by the Veterans of the Abraham Lincoln Brigade in 1951) indicates the extent of Hemingway's influence on the public perception of that war:

> It was felt that Hemingway's talent and the personal support he rendered to many phases of the loyalist cause were shockingly betrayed in

---

* 30 August 1935; *The Only Thing That Counts,* ed. Matthew J. Bruccoli (New York: Scribners, 1996), 224.
† "The Starched Blue Sky of Spain," *Noble Savage,* no. 1 (Spring 1960): 93.

his work "For Whom the Bell Tolls" in which the Spanish people were cruelly misrepresented and leaders of the International Brigade maliciously slandered. The novel in its total impact presented an unforgivable distortion of the meaning of the struggle in Spain. Under the name and prestige of Hemingway, important aid was given to humanity's worst enemies.*

IV

Hemingway's introductions, forewords, and prefaces are about Hemingway. The work he is ostensibly discussing provides an occasion for him to demonstrate his expertise in that field. His claims are sometimes embarrassing. A writer is his own fault. He is also the fault of readers who expect or require writers to be romantic or glamorous or self-destructive figures. Celebrity writers learn that they can get away with almost anything; and this realization spoils or ruins many of them. Hemingway gave the customers what they wanted and thereby cultivated the Hemingway legend.

The self-legendizing process in these personal writings functioned through style and language that depart from the controlled prose and understatement of Hemingway's books. Here the writing sometimes resembles parody Hemingway—what James Gould Cozzens called "that dreadful phony 'simplicity' of style."† It is even oracular, as in the nature-mysticism of "On the American Dead in Spain": "This spring the dead will feel the earth beginning to live again. . . . And as long as all our dead live in the Spanish earth, and they will live as long as the earth lives, no system of tyranny ever will prevail in Spain." Hemingway used sarcasm in his opinion pieces to attack and destroy the opposition. The targets are the fools and weaklings themselves, as well as their thinking and conduct. His weapon of choice was the ad hominem wisecrack.

Hemingway claimed that his influence on American prose was "only a certain clarification of the language which is now in public domain." There was more to it: he opened serious fiction to material that had been relegated to sub-literary status. He customarily assessed writers in the terminology of sports: "Imagine not being able to get your fastball by Truman Capote or dropping a close decision to some Brooklyn Tolstoy." Eleven of the pieces in this volume treat sport. Hemingway was probably the only writer who could have persuaded Americans who had never witnessed a bullfight that bullfighting was an ethical and aesthetic spectacle. More than any other writer, Ernest

* Alvah Bessie, *The Heart of Spain* (New York: Veterans of the Abraham Lincoln Brigade, 1951), vi.
† 18 May 1964; *Selected Notebooks: 1960–1967*, ed. Matthew J. Bruccoli (Columbia and Bloomfield Hills: Bruccoli Clark, 1984), 83.

Hemingway influenced what American writers were able to write about and the words they used.

The chronological organization of this volume traces the progress of Ernest Hemingway's megalomania. By the Fifties—probably earlier—his efforts to maintain his legends and roles had subverted his creative powers. He continued to write, but his work was self-indulgent and read like imitation Hemingway. John O'Hara diagnosed the malady of Hemingway's fame in a 1960 letter to William Maxwell:

> We have in Hemingway the most important writer of our time and the most important writer since Shakespeare. That is the statement I made in the famous Sunday Times review of ACROSS THE RIVER AND INTO THE TREES. The various circumstances that have made him the most important are not all of a purely literary nature. Some are anything but. We start with a first-rate, original, conscientious artist, who caught on because of his excellence. The literary and then the general public very quickly realized that a great artist was functioning in our midst. Publicity grew and grew, and Hemingway helped it to grow, not always deliberately but sometimes deliberately. He had an unusual, almost comical name; he was a big, strong, highly personable man. He associated himself, through his work, with big things: Africa, Italy, Spain, war, hunting, fishing, bullfighting, The Novel, Style, death, violence, castration, and a teasing remoteness from his homeland and from the lit'ry life. All these things make you think of Hemingway, and each and all of them add to his importance, that carries over from one writing job to another. I have a theory that there has not been a single issue of the Sunday Times book section in the past twenty years that has failed to mention Hemingway; his name is a synonym for writer with millions of people who have never read any work of fiction. Etc., etc. He is the father image of writing as FDR was of politics.
>
> Now this has not all been good for Hemingway, and Lord Acton's remark about power can be applied here, substituting acclaim for power. It is not good for any artist if he does not keep on working as, for example, Picasso has kept on working. The test of the man, and possibly of the artist, is what he does after he gets the Nobel prize. Hemingway, I'm afraid, has not done well in that test. It is not only that he has rested on his laureate; he might have done better to have rested. I am told, but I do not quite believe it, that he has several novels in a bank vault. I believed it for a while—until I saw the Life pieces*. I now believe that he has been wasting his time, which would be okay if he had

* "The Dangerous Summer," Life 49 (5, 12, 19 September 1960).

decided to quit, to decide that he wanted to write no more, and stuck to that decision. But there is a cheapness about Hemingway that I deplore. He likes to get a favorable mention in Leonard Lyons's column, which is cheapness at its cheapest, and extremely costly to the man who is willing to settle for it. Hemingway can't stand the quiet of retirement, and he can't stand the company of the ass-kissers with whom he deliberately surrounds himself. They don't realize that you can't win with Hemingway. He will give you an argument on anything, and he hates you just as much for arguing with him as he does for agreeing with him; and yet he can't reject the toadies. He comes to New York, makes an ass of himself with Earl Wilson and Toots Shor, then hurries away to what? To watch bullfighting and, later, to write about what is to me the most disgusting spectacle in modern sports-entertainment. But the worst spectacle in the Life pieces was not the bullfighting itself but the collapse of Ernest Hemingway, artist and man.*

For most of his professional life Ernest Hemingway was an undiagnosed manic-depressive—with alcoholism, which deteriorated his ability to control that condition. There is a poly-genetic predisposition for manic-depressive illness (bi-polar disorder), and it carries a high prevalence of suicide: there were four suicides in the Hemingway family. Manic-depression usually kicks in between fifteen and the late twenties, and it can be triggered by post-traumatic stress. Hemingway was nineteen when he was wounded in World War I; but he was already an ardent self-fabulist. The progress of Hemingway's manic-depressions can be traced through the evidence assembled here. After a certain point in the Thirties he may not have known when he was improving on the Ernest Hemingway saga.

---

* 23 September 1960; *Selected Letters of John O'Hara,* ed. Matthew J. Bruccoli (New York: Random House, 1978), pp. 348–349.

Chronology

21 July 1899	Ernest Miller Hemingway is born to Dr. Clarence Edmonds Hemingway and Grace Hall Hemingway in Oak Park, Illinois.
September 1915	EH begins writing for his high school newspaper, the *Trapeze,* and its literary magazine, the *Tabula.*
October 1917	EH takes a job as a cub reporter on the *Kansas City Star.*
Spring 1918	EH enlists with American Red Cross to drive ambulances in Italy.
8 July 1918	While passing out cigarettes and chocolate to Italian soldiers, EH is wounded by a trench mortar shell.
January–May 1920	EH is in Toronto, where he is freelance journalist for the *Toronto Star.*
December 1920	In Chicago EH begins writing for and editing the magazine *Cooperative Commonwealth.*
3 September 1921	EH marries Hadley Richardson.
8 December 1921	EH and Hadley Hemingway board ship for France. She has income from a trust fund, and he has freelance assignments from the *Toronto Star* for articles on Europe. They arrive in France on 20 December and remain in Europe until fall 1923.
6 July 1923	Hemingways make their first visit to the Fiesta of San Fermin and the bullfights at Pamplona, Spain, which provides material for *The Sun Also Rises.*
13 August 1923	*Three Stories and Ten Poems* is published in Paris by Robert McAlmon's Contact Editions.
10 October 1923	Hemingways return to Toronto, where he works as a reporter. Hadley Hemingway gives birth to John Hadley Nicanor Hemingway (Bumby).
30 January 1924	Hemingways return to France, where EH assists Ford Madox Ford as an editor and writer for the *Transatlantic Review.*

Early April 1924	*in our time,* a collection of vignettes, is published in Paris by William Bird's Three Mountains Press.
June–July 1925	Hemingways and friends are again in Pamplona, Spain, for the bullfights and the Fiesta of San Fermin. This visit provides further material for *The Sun Also Rises.*
5 October 1925	*In Our Time,* a collection of short stories and vignettes, is published in New York by Boni & Liveright.
11 February 1926	EH confers with Maxwell Perkins at Charles Scribner's Sons and begins his lifelong relationship with the publishing house.
28 May 1926	*The Torrents of Spring* is published by Scribners.
22 October 1926	*The Sun Also Rises* is published by Scribners.
14 April 1927	Hadley Richardson Hemingway and EH are divorced.
10 May 1927	EH marries heiress Pauline Pfeiffer.
14 October 1927	*Men Without Women,* a short-story collection, is published by Scribners.
28 June 1928	Pauline Hemingway gives birth to Patrick Hemingway in Kansas City.
May–October 1929	*A Farewell to Arms* is serialized in *Scribner's Magazine.*
27 September 1929	*A Farewell to Arms* is published by Scribners. The book elicits excellent reviews and sales.
12 November 1931	Pauline Hemingway gives birth to Gregory Hemingway in Kansas City.
23 September 1932	*Death in the Afternoon* is published by Scribners. The book has disappointing reviews and sales.
April 1933	EH agrees to write "Letters" for Arnold Gingrich's *Esquire.* He eventually publishes twenty-five articles and six short stories in the magazine.
27 October 1933	*Winner Take Nothing,* a short-story collection, is published by Scribners.
10 December 1933– 28 February 1934	Hemingways go on African safari that will provide material for *Green Hills of Africa* and two of EH's best-known stories, "The Short Happy Life of Francis Macomber" and "The Snows of Kilimanjaro."
May 1934	EH purchases his fishing boat, the *Pilar.*
May–November 1935	*Green Hills of Africa* is serialized in *Scribner's Magazine.*
25 October 1935	*Green Hills of Africa* is published by Scribners. The book has disappointing reviews and sales.

November 1936	EH is hired by North American Newspaper Alliance (NANA) to cover the Spanish Civil War; he helps with movie *Spain in Flames*.
Late December 1937	EH meets reporter Martha Gellhorn in Key West.
4 June 1937	EH delivers an address, "Fascism Is a Lie," at the American Writers Congress in New York. The speech is published in the 22 June issue of *New Masses*.
5 July 1937	Documentary film *The Spanish Earth*, narrated by EH, premieres in New York City.
15 October 1937	*To Have and Have Not* is published by Scribners. The book receives mixed reviews.
18 October 1937	EH appears for the first time on the cover of *Time*.
14 October 1938	*The Fifth Column and the First Forty-nine Stories* is published by Scribners.
April 1939	EH moves into La Finca Vigía near Havana, Cuba, with Martha Gellhorn.
7 March 1940	*The Fifth Column* opens on Broadway. Reviews are disappointing.
3 June 1940	*The Fifth Column: A Play in Three Acts* is published by Scribners.
21 October 1940	*For Whom the Bell Tolls* is published by Scribners. The book elicits excellent reviews and sales.
4 November 1940	Pauline Pfeiffer Hemingway and EH are divorced.
21 November 1940	EH marries Martha Gellhorn.
11 February– 6 May 1941	Hemingway and Gellhorn go to China to cover the war there.
January 1942– April 1944	Martha Gellhorn covers European war for *Collier's*. EH remains in Cuba, where he hunts for German submarines with the *Pilar*.
October 1942	*Men at War*, an anthology edited and with a preface by EH, is published in New York by Crown.
May 1944	EH accepts assignment to cover European war for *Collier's*. Spends most of his time until March 1945 in France.
21 December 1945	Martha Gellhorn and EH are divorced.
January 1946	EH is working on material that will be published as *The Garden of Eden*.
14 March 1946	EH marries Mary Welsh.

November 1948   EH is working on material that will become *Islands in the Stream.*

April 1949   EH is working on material that will become *Across the River and Into the Trees.*

February–June 1950   *Across the River and Into the Trees* is serialized in *Cosmopolitan.*

7 September 1950   *Across the River and Into the Trees* is published by Scribners. The book receives mostly unfavorable reviews.

1 September 1952   *The Old Man and the Sea* is published in *Life.* More than five million copies of the issue are printed.

8 September 1952   *The Old Man and the Sea* is published by Scribners.

May 1953   *The Old Man and the Sea* wins the Pulitzer Prize.

1 September 1953–
21 January 1954   The Hemingways go on African safari.

23 January 1954   During flight to Murchison Falls, the Hemingways' plane crashes. Though everyone onboard survives, newspapers throughout the world report EH's death.

24 January 1954   A second plane taking the Hemingways to Entebbe bursts into flames on takeoff. EH is injured, but the entire party again survives.

28 October 1954   EH is awarded the Nobel Prize for Literature. Pleading ill health, he has American ambassador John Cabot read his acceptance speech at the 11 December Nobel ceremonies in Stockholm.

April 1956   EH works on African book that becomes *True at First Light.*

September 1957   EH works on memoir that will become *A Moveable Feast.*

January–July 1958   In Cuba EH works on material for *A Moveable Feast* and *The Garden of Eden.*

1–2 January 1959   Castro overthrows Batista government, and EH leaves Cuba for Ketchum, Idaho.

Summer 1959   Hemingways are in Spain, where EH follows matadors Antonio Ordóñez and Luis Miguel Domínguín and collects material for *Life* that will become *The Dangerous Summer.*

May 1960   EH delivers 120,000-word typescript to *Life,* which had asked for a 10,000-word article. Three installments of *The Dangerous Summer* are published in the magazine during September.

30 November 1960   EH enters Mayo Clinic, Rochester, Minnesota, suffering from paranoia, depression, hypertension, and diabetes. Undergoes electroshock therapy in December 1960 and January 1961. In Ketchum he twice attempts suicide in April 1961 and returns to the Mayo Clinic for two months of treatment.

2 July 1961   Two days after he comes home to Ketchum, EH kills himself with his shotgun.

5 May 1964   *A Moveable Feast* is published by Scribners.

6 October 1970   *Islands in the Stream* is published by Scribners.

24 June 1985   *The Dangerous Summer* is published by Scribners.

28 May 1986   *The Garden of Eden* is published by Scribners.

21 July 1999   *True at First Light,* edited by Patrick Hemingway, is published by Scribners.

Hemingway and
the Mechanism of Fame

Review of *Batouala* (Paris: A. Michel, 1921) by René Maran,
Toronto Star Weekly, 25 March 1922, 3.

Hemingway's first book review was written as a news article when he was a
Toronto Star *stringer in Paris. He probably read the English-language trans-*
lation (New York: Thomas Seltzer, 1922).

Paris.—"Batouala," the novel by René Maran, a Negro, winner of the Goncourt Academy Prize of 5,000 francs for the best novel of the year by a young
writer, is still the center of a swirl of condemnation, indignation and praise.

Maran, who was born in Martinique and educated in France, was bitterly
attacked in the Chamber of Deputies the other day as a defamer of France,
and biter of the hand that fed him. He has been much censured by certain
Frenchmen for his indictment of French imperialism in its effects on the
natives of the French colonies. Others have rallied to him and asked the politicians to take the novel as a work of art, except for the preface, which is the
only bit of propaganda in the book.

Meanwhile, René Maran, black as Sam Langford [the boxer],[1] is ignorant
of the storm his book has caused. He is in the French government service in
Central Africa, two days' march from Lake Tchad, and seventy days' travel
from Paris. There are no telegraphs or cables at his post, and he does not even
know his book has won the famous Goncourt Prize.

The preface of the novel describes how peaceful communities of 10,000
blacks in the heart of Africa have been reduced to 1,000 inhabitants under the
French rule. It is not pleasant and it gives the facts by a man who has seen
them, in a plain, unimpassioned statement.

Launched into the novel itself, the reader gets a picture of a native village
seen by the big-whited eyes, felt by the pink palms, and the broad, flat, naked
feet of the African native himself. You smell the smells of the village, you eat
its food, you see the white man as the black man sees him, and after you have
lived in the village you die there. That is all there is to the story, but when you
have read it, you have seen Batouala, and that makes it a great novel.

It opens with Batouala, the chief of the village, waking up in his hut,
roused by the cold of the early morning and the crumbling of the ground
under his body where the ants are tunneling. He blows his dead fire into life

and sits, hunched over, warming his chilled body and wondering whether he will go back to sleep or get up.

It closes with Batouala, old and with the stiffened joints of his age, cruelly torn by the leopard that his spear-thrust missed, lying on the earth floor of his hut. The village sorcerer has left him alone, there is a younger chief in the village, and Batouala lies there feverish and thirsty, dying, while his mangy dog licks at his wounds. And while he lies there, you feel the thirst and the fever and the rough, moist tongue of the dog.

There will probably be an English translation shortly. To be translated properly, however, there should be another Negro who has lived a life in the country two days' march from Lake Tchad and who knows English as René Maran knows French.

1. Thus in published text.

Front cover of the novel that was the subject of Hemingway's first book review. Location: *Hemingway in Africa: The Last Safari* by Christopher Ondaatje (Woodstock & New York: Overlook Press, 2004), 26. Thomas Cooper Library, University of South Carolina.

"Conrad, Optimist and Moralist," *Transatlantic Review* 2 (October 1924): 341–42. Location: C. E. Frazer Clark Collection, University of Maryland Libraries.

Joseph Conrad died 3 August 1924. Hemingway's tribute is personal, as are all of his literary statements. This article appeared in the issue of Ford Madox Ford's Transatlantic Review *that Hemingway edited in Ford's absence. Hemingway's ridicule of Eliot occasioned a public apology by Ford, which exacerbated Hemingway's dislike of Ford. The other contributors to this memorial to Conrad were American writer Robert McAlmon and British novelist Ethel Mayne.*

What is there you can write about him now that he is dead?

The critics will dive into their vocabularies and come up with articles on the death of Conrad. They are diving now, like prairie dogs.

It will not be hard for the editorial writers; Death of John L. Sullivan, Death of Roosevelt, Death of Major Whittlesey, Death of President Coolidge's Son, Death of Honored Citizen, Passing of Pioneer, Death of President Wilson, Great Novelist Passes, it is all the same.

CONRAD, OPTIMIST AND MORALIST

Admirers of Joseph Conrad, whose sudden death is an occasion for general regret, usually think of him as an artist of the first rank, as a remarkable story teller and as a stylist. But Mr. Conrad was also a deep thinker and serene philosopher. In his novels, as in his essays etc.

It will run like that. All over the country.

And what is there that you can say about him now that he is dead?

It is fashionable among my friends to disparage him. It is even necessary. Living in a world of literary politics where one wrong opinion often proves fatal, one writes carefully. I remember how I was made to feel how easily one might be dropped from the party, and the short period of Coventry that followed my remarking when speaking of George Antheil that I preferred my Stravinsky straight. I have been more careful since.

It is agreed by most of the people I know that Conrad is a bad writer, just as it is agreed that T. S. Eliot is a good writer. If I knew that by grinding Mr. Eliot into a fine dry powder and sprinkling that powder over Mr. Conrad's grave Mr. Conrad would shortly appear, looking very annoyed at the forced return and commence writing I would leave for London early tomorrow morning with a sausage grinder.

One should not be funny over the death of a great man, but you cannot couple T. S. Eliot and Joseph Conrad in a sentence seriously any more than you could see, say, André Germain and Manuel Garcia (Maera)[1] walking down the street together and not laugh.

The second book of Conrad's that I read was *Lord Jim*. I was unable to finish it. It is, therefore, all I have left of him. For I cannot re-read them. That may be what my friends mean by saying he is a bad writer. But from nothing else that I have ever read have I gotten what every book of Conrad has given me.

Knowing I could not re-read them I saved up four that I would not read until I needed them badly, when the disgust with writing, writers and everything written of and to write would be too much. Two months in Toronto used up the four books. One after another I borrowed them from a girl who had all of his books on a shelf, bound in blue leather, and had never read any of them. Let us be exact. She had read *The Arrow of Gold* and *Victory*.

In Sudbury, Ontario, I bought three back numbers of the *Pictorial Review* and read *The Rover*, sitting up in bed in the Nickle Range Hotel. When morning came I had used up all my Conrad like a drunkard, I had hoped it would last me the trip, and felt like a young man who has blown in his patrimony. But, I thought, he will write more stories. He has lots of time.

When I read the reviews they all agreed *The Rover* was a bad story.

And now he is dead and I wish to God they would have taken some great, acknowledged technician of a literary figure and left him to write his bad stories.

1. Germain was a French literary critic whose books included one on D'Annunzio's love life; Maera was the Spanish bullfighter whom Hemingway most admired. His comparison of the two men is meant to be ludicrous.

"Homage to Ezra," *This Quarter* 1 (Spring 1925): 221–25.

Ezra Pound (1885–1972), one of the important writers who helped Hemingway during his early Paris years, was the only one of the benefactors who escaped his contempt. (Hemingway remained an admirer of James Joyce, but Joyce had not helped him.) Although Hemingway later claimed that Pound had not edited his early work, Pound had encouraged him and had arranged for publication of in our time. *Hemingway later stated: "Ezra was right half the time, and when he was wrong he was so wrong you were never in any doubt about it. Gertrude [Stein (1874–1946)] was always right."*[1] *Hemingway remained loyal to Pound; four items in this volume celebrate Pound as a great poet.*

An editor has written asking me to write an appreciation of Ezra Pound, to be written as though Pound were dead. One does not write appreciations of dead men but only of their work. Dead men themselves are most uncomfortable to have around and sooner or later one buries them or walks behind them to where others bury them or reads about their funeral in the newspaper and perhaps sends telegrams in which it is impossible to avoid clichés. And if one tries to write about dead men who were one's friends one fails for one reason or another and it is no good.

Stylists can do it because they have a way of wrapping things around in the style like *emballeurs* or the men who wrapped mummies in Egypt. Even stylists though do it only to their own satisfaction. No one else is very pleased.

So thank God Pound isn't dead and we don't have to write about him as though he were.

Ezra Pound devotes perhaps one fifth of his working time to writing poetry and in this twenty per cent of effort writes a large and distinguished share of the really great poetry that has been written by any American living or dead— or any Englishman living or dead or any Irishman who ever wrote English. I do not mention other nationalities because I do not know the poetry of other countries nor do I know Gaelic. There is only one living poet who ranks with Pound and that is William Butler Yeats. Some of Pound's later manner is done better by T. S. Eliot. But Eliot is, after all, a minor poet. Just as Marianne Moore is a minor poet and Wallace Stevens is a minor poet. Fine poetry is written by minor poets.

Pound happens to be a major poet just as Yeats is and Browning and Shelley and Keats were. What is the difference? It seems hardly necessary to point it out but it is easier to do through the case of Eliot. All of Eliot's poems are perfect and there are very few of them. He has a very fine talent and he is very careful of it. He never takes chances with it and it is doing very well thank you. Whitman, on the other hand, if a poet, is a major poet.

The most perfect poem to me in the *Oxford Book of English Verse* was written by Anonymous. Yet I have to consider Anonymous a minor poet because if he were a major poet there would have been a name to him. That may sound like Dr. Frank Crane. But take A. E. Houseman. There is the perfect case of the minor poet. He did it once and did it perfectly with the *Shropshire Lad* but when he tried to do again it wouldn't come off and the trick of mind all showed through and it imperilled the poems in the first book. One more book would have killed off all the poems. They proved to be unimportant.

Minor poets do not fail because they do not attempt the major thing. They have nothing of major importance to say. They do a minor thing with perfection and the perfection is admirable. Ezra has written great poetry.

This is an appreciation rather than a critical article. If it were the latter I would have to stop here and go up to Paris to verify quotations. There ought to be quotations if this were to prove anything. Fortunately an appreciation does not have to prove anything.

So then, so far, we have Pound the major poet devoting, say, one fifth of his time to poetry. With the rest of his time he tries to advance the fortunes, both material and artistic, of his friends. He defends them when they are attacked, he gets them into magazines and out of jail. He loans them money. He sells their pictures. He arranges concerts for them. He writes articles about them. He introduces them to wealthy women. He gets publishers to take their books. He sits up all night with them when they claim to be dying and he witnesses their wills. He advances them hospital expenses and dissuades them from suicide. And in the end a few of them refrain from knifing him at the first opportunity.

Personally he is tall, has a patchy red beard, fine eyes, strange haircuts and is very shy. But he has the temperament of a *toro di lidia* from the breeding establishments of Don Eduardo Miura. No one ever presents a cape, or shakes a muleta at him without getting a charge. Like Don Eduardo's product too he sometimes ignores the picador's horse to pick off the man and no one goes into the ring with him in safety. And though they can always be sure of drawing his charge yet he gets his quota of bull-baiters each year.

Many people hate him and he plays a fine game of tennis. He would live much longer if he did not eat so fast. Young men in the years after the war coming over from America where Pound was a legendary person to Paris where they found him with a patchy red beard, very accessible, fond of tennis and occasionally playing the bassoon, decided there could not be anything in the Pound legend and that he was probably not a great poet after all. As the army rhyme used to say: hence criticism in America.

Like all men who become famous very young he suffers from not being read. It is so much easier to talk about a classic than to read it. There is another generation, though, in America that is replacing the generation that decided Ezra could not be a great poet because he was actually alive and kicking, and this generation is reading him. They come to Paris now and want to meet him. But he has gone to Italy.

As he takes no interest in Italian politics and does not mind Italian cookery he may stay there sometime. It is good for him to be there because his friends cannot get at him so easily and energy is thus released for production. Pound is among other things a composer and has done a splendid opera on Villon. It is a first rate opera. A very fine opera.

But I feel about Ezra and music something like about M. Constantin Brancusi and cooking. M. Brancusi is a famous sculptor who is also a very famous cook. Cooking is, of course, an art it would be lamentable if M. Brancusi would give up sculpture for it or even devote the major part of his time to cookery.

Still Ezra is not a minor poet. He has never been troubled by lack of energy. If he wants to write more operas he will write them and there will be plenty of force left over.

As this is an appreciation there is one thing to be emphasized about Ezra. He has never been a pitiful figure. He has fought his fights with a very gay

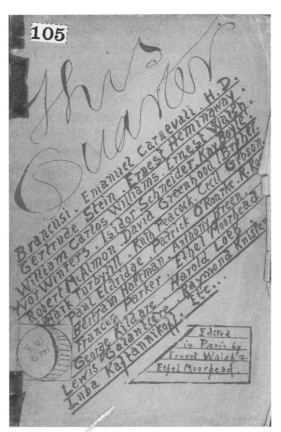

Front cover of the Paris magazine in which both this tribute to Pound and Hemingway's "Big Two-Hearted River" first appeared. Location: Speiser and Easterling-Hallman Foundation Collection of Ernest Hemingway, Thomas Cooper Library, University of South Carolina.

grimness and his wounds heal quickly. He does not believe that he came into the world to suffer. He is no masochist and that is one more reason why he is not a minor poet.

1. John Peale Bishop, "Homage to Hemingway," *New Republic* 89 (11 November 1936): 39–42.

Review of *A Story-Teller's Story* (New York: Huebsch, 1924) by Sherwood Anderson, *Ex Libris* 2 (March 1925): 176–77. Location: Matthew J. and Arlyn Bruccoli Collection of F. Scott Fitzgerald, Thomas Cooper Library, University of South Carolina.

Hemingway's review appeared—with a companion review by Gertrude Stein —in Ex Libris, *the journal of the American Library in Paris. Written fourteen months before publication of Hemingway's parody of Anderson,* The Torrents of Spring—*but before Hemingway had read* Dark Laughter *(1925)—his review mixes praise for Anderson's tales with distrust of his literary friends whose influence resulted in the failure of* Many Marriages *(New York: Huebsch, 1923).*

In a review of Ernest Hemingway's "In Our Time" (The Three Mountain Press) the *Dial* recently said: "Mr. Hemingway's poems are not particularly important, but his prose is of the first distinction. He must be counted as the only American writer but one—Mr. Sherwood Anderson—who has felt the genius of Gertrude Stein's 'Three Lives' and has been evidently influenced by it. Indeed Miss Stein, Mr. Anderson and Mr. Hemingway may now be said to form a school by themselves." Two of these writers have consented to give *Ex Libris* their opinion in regard to the latest book written by the third.

THE EDITOR.

The reviewers have all compared this book with the "Education of Henry Adams" and it was not hard for them to do so, for Sherwood Anderson twice refers to the Adams book and there is plenty in the "Story Teller's Story" about the cathedral at Chartres. Evidently the Education book made a deep impression on Sherwood for he quotes part of it. He also has a couple of other learned quotations in Latin and I can imagine him copying them on the typewriter verifying them carefully to get the spelling right. For Sherwood Anderson, unlike the English, does not quote you Latin in casual conversation.

As far as I know the Latin is correct although English reviewers may find flaws in it, and all of my friends own and speak of "The Education of Henry Adams" with such solemnity that I have been unable ever to read it. "A Story Teller's Story" is a good book. It is such a good book that it doesn't need to be coupled in the reviewing with Henry Adams or anybody else.

This is the Life and Times of Sherwood Anderson and a great part of it runs along in a mildly kidding way as though Sherwood were afraid people would think he took himself and his life too seriously. But there is no joking about the way he writes of horses and women and bartenders and Judge Turner and the elder Berners and the half allegorical figure of the poor devil of a magazine writer who comes in at the end of the book. And if Sherwood jokes about the base-ball player beating him up at the warehouse where he worked, you get at the same time, a very definite sharp picture of the baseball player, drunk, sullen and amazed, knocking him down as soon and as often as he got up while the two teamsters watched and wondered why this fellow named Anderson had picked a fight when he couldn't fight.

There are very beautiful places in the book, as good writing as Sherwood Anderson has done and that means considerably better than any other American writer has done. It is a great mystery and an even greater tribute to Sherwood that so many people writing today think he cannot write. They believe that he has very strange and sometimes beautiful ideas and visions and that he expresses them very clumsily and unsuccessfully. While in reality he often takes a very banal idea of things and presents it with such craftsmanship that the person reading believes it beautiful and does not see the craftsmanship at all. When he calls himself "a poor scribbler" don't believe him.

He is not a poor scribbler even though he calls himself that or worse, again and again. He is a very great writer and if he has at times, in other books been unsuccessful, it has been for two reasons. His talent and his development of it has been toward the short story or tale and not toward that highly artificial form the novel. The second reason is that he has been what the French say of all honest politicians *mal entouré*.

In "A Story Teller's Story," which is highly successful as a piece of work because it is written in his own particular form, a series of short tales jointed up sometimes and sometimes quite disconnected, he pays homage to his New York friends who have helped him. They nearly all took something from him, and tried to give him various things in return that he needed as much as a boxer needs diamond studded teeth. And because he gave them all something he is, after the manner of all great men, very grateful to them. They called him a "phallic Chekov" and other meaningless things and watched for the sparkle of his diamond studded teeth and Sherwood got a little worried and uncertain and wrote a poor book called "Many Marriages." Then all the people who hated him because he was an American who could write and did write and had been given a prize and was starting to have some success jumped on him with loud cries that he never had written and never would be able to write and if you didn't believe it read "Manny Marriages." Now Sherwood has written a fine book and they are all busy comparing him to Henry Adams.

Anyway you ought to read "A Story Teller's Story." It is a wonderful comeback after "Many Marriages."

Petition, "A Protest against Pirating 'Ulysses,'" *New York Herald Tribune Books,* **6 March 1927, 21.**

James Joyce's Ulysses *was published by Sylvia Beach's Paris bookshop, Shakespeare and Company, in 1922 but was banned from distribution or publication in America on the basis of its alleged indecency. Samuel Roth, an egregious American literary pirate, began publishing an unauthorized serialization of* Ulysses *in his* Two Worlds Monthly *in 1926, as well as bootleg copies of the book. Supported by this petition, Joyce brought suit against Roth, who was forced to cease publication of* Ulysses *in the fall of 1927.*

Correspondence

A Protest Against Pirating "Ulysses"

To the Editor of "Books":

It is a matter of common knowledge that the "Ulysses" of Mr. James Joyce is being republished in the United States, in a magazine edited by Samuel Roth, and that this republication is being made without authorization by Mr. Joyce, without payment to Mr. Joyce and with alterations which seriously corrupt the text. This appropriation and mutilation of Mr. Joyce's property are made under color of legal protection in that the "Ulysses" which is published in France and which has been excluded from the mails in the United States is not protected by copyright in the United States. The question of justification of that exclusion is not now in issue; similar decisions have been made by government officials with reference to works of art before this. The question in issue is whether the public (including the editors and publishers to whom his advertisements are offered) will encourage Mr. Samuel Roth to take advantage of the resultant legal difficulty of the author to deprive him of his property and to mutilate the creation of his art. The undersigned protest against Mr. Roth's conduct in republishing "Ulysses" and appeal to the American public, in the name of that security of works of the intellect and the imagination without which art cannot live, to oppose to Mr. Roth's enterprise the full power of honorable and fair opinion.

(Signed)

full power of honorable and fair opinion.

(Signed)

Lascelles Abercrombie
Richard Aldington
Sherwood Anderson
René Arcos
M. Arcybacheff
Ebba Atterbom
Azorin
C. du Baissauray
Léon Bazalgette
Jacinto Benavente
Silvio Benco
Julien Benda
Arnold Bennett
J. Benoist-Méchin
Konrad Bercovici
J. D. Beresford
Rudolf Binding
M. Bontempelli
Jean de Bosschère
Ivan Bounine
  l'Académie Russe
Robert Bridges
Eugène Brieux
  l'Acad. Française
Bryher
Olaf Bull
Mary Butts
Louis Cazamian
Jacques Chenevière
Abel Chevalley
M. Constan.-Wéyer
Albert Crémieux
Benjamin Crémieux
Benedetto Croce
Ernst R. Curtius
Francis Dickie
H. D.
Norman Douglas
Charles Du Bos
Georges Duhamel
Edouard Dujardin
Luc Durtain
Albert Einstein
T. S. Eliot
Havelock Ellis
Edouard Estaunié
  l'Acad. Française
Léon-Paul Fargue
E. M. Forster
François Fosca
Gaston Gallimard
Edward Garnett
Giovanni Gentile
André Gide
Philip Gibbs
Bernard Gilbert
Ivan Goll
R. G. de la Serna
Cora Gordon
Jan Gordon
Georg Goyert
Alice S. Green
Julian Green
Augusta Gregory
Daniel Halévy
Knut Hamsun
Jane Harrison
H. L. Hartley
Ernest Hemingway
H. v. Hofmannsthal
Sisley Huddleston
Stephen Hudson
George F. Hummel
Bampton Hunt
Bravig Imbs
Holbrook Jackson
Edmond Jaloux
Storm Jameson
Juan Ramon Jimenez
Eugène Jolas
Henry Festing Jones
George Kaiser
Hermann Keyserling
Manuel Komroff
A. Kouprine

René Lalou
Pierre de Lanux
Valery Larbaud
D. H. Lawrence
Emile Legouis
Wyndham Lewis
Ludwig Lewisohn
Victor Llona
Mina Loy
Archibald MacLeish
Brinsley MacNamara
Maurice Maeterlinck
Thomas Mann
Antonio Marichalar
Dora Marsden
John Masefield
W. S. Maugham
André Maurois
D. Merejkovsky
Régis Michaud
Gabriel Miro
Hope Mirrlees
T. Sturge Moore
Paul Morand
Auguste Morel
Arthur Moss
J. Middleton Murry
Sean O'Casey
Liam O'Flaherty
Jose Ortega y Gasset
Seumas O'Sullivan
Elliot H. Paul
Jean Paulhan
Arthur Pinero
Luigi Pirandello
Jean Prévost
Marcel Prévost
  de l'Académie Française
C. F. Ramuz
Alfonso Reyes
Ernest Rhys
Elmer E. Rice
Dorothy Richardson
Jac. Robertfrance
Lennox Robinson
John Rodker
Romain Rolland
Jules Romains
Bertrand Russell
G. W. Russell "A.E."
Ludmilla Savitzky
Jean Schlumberger
May Sinclair
W. L. Smyser
E. Œ. Somerville
Philippe Soupault
André Spire
Th. Stephanides
André Suares
Italo Svevo
Frank Swinnerton
Arthur Symons
Marcel Thiébaut
Virgil Thomson
Robert de Traz
R. C. Trevelyan
Miguel de Unamuno
Laurence Vail
Paul Valéry
  de l'Académie Française
Fernand Vandérem
Fritz Vanderpyl
Francis Viélé-Griffin
Hugh Walpole
Jacob Wassermann
H. G. Wells
Rebecca West
Anna Wickham
Thornton Wilder
Robert Wolf
Virginia Woolf
W. B. Yeats

Paris, Feb. 2, 1927.

Excerpt from Letter in "Behind the Scenes," *Scribner's Magazine* 81 (March 1927): 4.

Hemingway's "The Killers" was published in this issue—his first short-story publication in America. His statement is accompanied by the incorrect editorial information that "he was severely wounded while serving with the Italian Arditi" and that he has "performed" in the bull ring.

Possibly the earliest caricature of Hemingway (*Vanity Fair* 29 [January 1928]: 78). Location: Speiser and Easterling-Hallman Foundation Collection of Ernest Hemingway, Thomas Cooper Library, University of South Carolina.

"There really is, to me anyway, very great glamor in life—and places and all sorts of things and I would like sometime to get it into the stuff. People aren't all as bad as some writers find them or as hollowed out and exhausted emotionally as some of The Sun generation. I've known some very wonderful people who even though they were going directly toward the grave (which is what makes any story a tragedy if carried out until the end) managed to put up a very fine performance en route."

Blurb on dust-jacket band for *Nothing Is Sacred* by Josephine Herbst (New York: Coward-McCann, 1928).

Herbst (1892–1969), a novelist and radical, was married to novelist John Herrmann (1900–1959); they were Hemingway's friends. This was Herbst's first book.

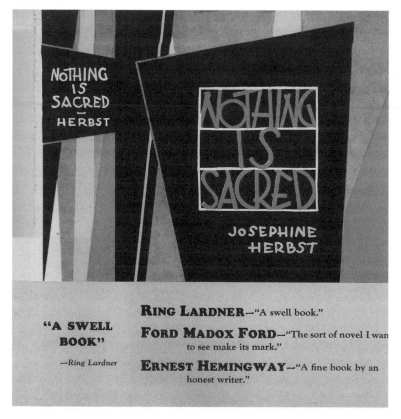

Location: Matthew J. and Arlyn Bruccoli Collection of F. Scott Fitzgerald, Thomas Cooper Library, University of South Carolina.

Letter to *Little Review* **12 (May 1929): 41. Location: Harry Ransom Humanities Research Center, University of Texas, Austin.**

Pound was poetry editor for Margaret Anderson and Jane Heap's Little Review, *which ceased publication with the May 1929 issue. Hemingway's letter accompanied his satirical poem "Valentine: For a Mr. Lee Wilson Dodd and Any of His Friends Who Want It." Dodd's 19 November 1927 assessment of* Men Without Women *in the* Saturday Review of Literature *praised Hemingway's style but criticized his "hard-boiled" subject matter. Hemingway's mention of the* Atlantic Monthly *refers to the 1927 publication of "Fifty Grand" in that magazine.*

Enclosed please find a piece for the Final Number of yr. esteemed weekly.

I hope this will meet with your qualifications that it should not be literature.

I have been working on this day and night since your letter came and wd. greatly enjoy your acknowledging receipt of same and whether you will use same as there is a great demand for my work by the Atlantic Monthly and kindred periodicals and wd. not like to disappoint these editors when I have a piece so immenently or emminently saleable.

Yrs. always,

HEM

This *Publishers' Weekly*
advertisement for the
Scribner's Magazine serialization of Hemingway's
third novel (May–October
1929) featured Helen
Breaker's photograph of
the young writer.

**Introduction to *Kiki of Montparnasse* (New York: Titus/Black Manikin
Press, 1929). Location: C. E. Frazer Clark Collection, University of Maryland
Libraries. Reprinted in *Kiki's Memoirs* (Paris: Titus/Black Manikin Press,
1930). Location: Speiser and Easterling-Hallman Foundation Collection of
Ernest Hemingway, Thomas Cooper LIbrary, University of South Carolina.**

*Kiki (Alice Prin, 1901–53) was a popular Paris artists' model and entertainer
during the Twenties. Hemingway's remark about "present day lady writers of
all sexes" is characteristic of his insistence on the relationship between sexual
activity and good writing. Kiki was the subject of widely reproduced photos
by Man Ray.*

There are enough photographs of Kiki in this book so you can have some idea how she looked in the ten years that are just over. This is being written in nineteen hundred and twenty-nine and Kiki now looks like a monument to herself and to the era of Montparnasse that was definitely marked as closed when she, Kiki, published this book.

Decades end every ten years dating from any original occurrence, such as the birth of Christ, or the end of the war, but eras can end any time. No one knows when they begin, at least not at the time, and the ones that are noted and advertised at the start usually do not stand up very long; the Era that was to start with Locarno, for instance.

An Era is easy to start in the newspapers; editorial writers start them regularly, but people forget all about them and they have nothing to do with real Eras. I hope no one will be rude enough at this point to consult a dictionary and find out what an Era really and exactly is because that might spoil all this big writing. The essential in big writing is to use words like the West, the East, Civilization, etc., and very often these words do not mean a damned thing but you cannot have big writing without them. My own experience has been that when you stand with your nose toward the north, if your head is held still, what is on your right will be east and what is on your left will be west and you can write very big putting those words in capitals but it is very liable not to mean anything.

However to get back to Eras, which is another big way of writing, although nobody knows when they start everybody is pretty sure when they are over and when, in one year, Kiki became monumental and Montparnasse became rich, prosperous, brightly lighted, dancing-ed, shredded-wheated, grape-nuts-ed or grapenutted (take your choice, gentlemen, we have all these breakfast foods now) and they sold caviar at the Dome, well, the Era for what it was worth, and personally I don't think it was worth much, was over.

Montparnasse for this purpose means the cafes and the restaurants where people are seen in public. It does not mean the apartments, studios and hotel rooms where they work in private. In the old days the difference between the workers and those that didn't work was that the bums could be seen at the cafes in the forenoon. This of course was not entirely true as the greatest bums, using the word in the American rather than in the English connotation, did not rise until about five o'clock when, on entering the cafes, they would drink in friendly competition with the workers who had just knocked off work for the day. The worker goes to the café with the lonesomeness that a writer or painter has after he has worked all day and does not want to think about it until the next day but instead see people and talk about anything that is not serious and drink a little before supper. And maybe during and after

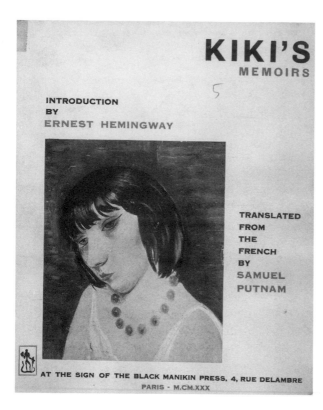

KIKI'S
MEMOIRS

INTRODUCTION
BY
ERNEST HEMINGWAY

TRANSLATED
FROM
THE
FRENCH
BY
SAMUEL
PUTNAM

AT THE SIGN OF THE BLACK MANIKIN PRESS, 4, RUE DELAMBRE
PARIS · M.CM.XXX

This book was published in New York and Paris with variant titles. The front cover of the 1930 Paris edition is illustrated here.

supper, too, depending on the individual. It was also very pleasant, after working, to see Kiki. She was very wonderful to look at. Having a fine face to start with she had made of it a work of art. She had a wonderfully beautiful body and a fine voice, talking voice, not singing voice, and she certainly dominated that era of Montparnasse more than Queen Victoria ever dominated the Victorian era.

The Era is over. It passed along with the kidneys of the workers who drank too long with the bums. The bums were fine people and proved to have the stronger kidneys finally. But then they rested during the day. Still that Era is over.

Kiki still has the voice. We do not have to worry about her kidneys, she comes from Burgundy where they make these things better than they do in Illinois or Massachusetts, and her face is as fine a work of art as ever. It is just that she has more material to work with now; but you have the photographs in the book and then you have the book. The book is supposed to be the point of this.

The people who tell me which books are great lasting works of art are all out of town so I cannot make an intelligent judgment, but I think Kiki's book is with the best I have read since The Enormous Room. Maybe it won't translate, but if it does not seem any good to you, learn French and read it. It won't hurt to learn to read French anyway and by then you will have forgotten all about this. But in case you do learn it, it was Kiki's book I said to read, not Julian Green's[1] nor Jean Cocteau's, nor whoever should be at that time great French writers for Americans. Read it all, from start to finish, the last chapter does not matter and does it no good, but you will not mind it after you have read Chapter VII called Initiation Manquee or Ma Grand'-mere which is Chapter XII.

This is the only book I have ever written an introduction for and, God help me, the only one I ever will. It is a crime to translate it. If it shouldn't be any good in English, and reading it just now again and seeing how it goes, I know it is going to be a bad job for whoever translates it, please read it in the original. It is written by a woman who, as far as I know, never had a Room of Her Own, but I think a part of it will remind you, and some of it will bear comparison with, another book with a woman's name written by Daniel Defoe. If you ever tire of books written by present day lady writers of all sexes, you have a book here written by a woman who was never a lady at any time. For about ten years she was about as close as people get nowadays to being a Queen but that, of course, is very different from being a lady.

1. "I have never read Mr. Green so this reference is probably very unjust. They tell me he is very good. So let me withdraw the advice, or rather change it to urge you after having learned French, to read *both* Kiki and Mr. Green."

"Who Knows How?" in *Creating the Short Story: A Symposium Anthology*, ed. Henry Goodman (New York: Harcourt, Brace, [1929]), 121. Location: Speiser and Easterling-Hallman Foundation Collection of Ernest Hemingway, Thomas Cooper Library, University of South Carolina.

This headnote for "The Killers" is Hemingway's first published account of his writing process. Goodman's anthology prints stories, with headnotes, by twenty-two writers; Hemingway's name appears on the title page with those of older, well-known story writers Wilbur Daniel Steele, Sherwood Anderson, Konrad Bercovici, Ring Lardner, and Zona Gale. His report characteristically utilizes details—the bus route and the names of the newspapers—to support the veracity of his memory.

For the guidance of your classes, the way in which I wrote a story called "The Undefeated" was as follows:

I got the idea of writing it while on an AE bus in Paris just as it was passing the Bon Marché (a large department store on the Boulevard Raspail). I was standing on the back platform of the bus and was in a great hurry to get home to start writing before I would lose it. I wrote all during lunch and until I was tired. Each succeeding day I went out of the house to a café in the morning and wrote on the story. It took several days to finish it. I do not remember the names of the cafés.

I wrote a story called "The Killers," in Madrid. I started it when I woke up after lunch and worked on it until supper. At supper I was very tired and drank a bottle of wine and read *La Voz, El Heraldo, Informaciones, El Debate* so as not to think about the story. After supper I went out for a walk. I saw no one I knew and went back to bed. The next morning I wrote a story called "Today Is Friday." I forget what we had for lunch. That afternoon it snowed.

My other stories have mostly been written in bed in the morning. If the above is not practical for the pupils perhaps they could substitute Fifth Avenue bus for AE bus; Saks for the Bon Marché; drug store for café—I believe there would be little difference except that they might not be permitted to write in a drug store.

Statement on Writing, *Modern Writers at Work,* **ed. Josephine K. Piercy (New York: Macmillan, 1930), 488–90. Location: Speiser and Easterling-Hallman Foundation Collection of Ernest Hemingway, Thomas Cooper Library, University of South Carolina.**

This anthology, which was also printed in a student edition, includes on page 489 a facsimile of a manuscript page from A Farewell to Arms. *Hemingway's comment on the relationship between writing and living is the headnote for his story "Cat in the Rain." In the table of contents Hemingway appears in a section titled "Among Eminent Short-Story Writers," in company with such authors as Katherine Mansfield, Sherwood Anderson, Edith Wharton, Wilbur Daniel Steele, and Irvin S. Cobb.*

Everyone writes prose badly to start but by continuing some get to write it well. Stop or go on is the only advice I know.

As for the practical side; I believe the typewriter is a curse of modern writing. It makes it too easy and the writing is solidified in type and is hard to change when it might still be kept plastic and be worked over and brought nearer to what it should be before it is cast in type. This all sounds very high flown but you must remember that you are asking some one engaged in a craft which he is constantly studying, practicing and trying to learn more about.

I should think it might take a lifetime to learn to write prose well; your own prose that is; for if it is not your own it is of no value. Then if you had spent your life doing it perhaps you would have nothing to write about.

The ideal way would be to live and then write or live and write at the same time. But it is very hard to serve two masters and a writer is very lucky if he has only two.

At any rate what we should avoid is developing a lot of completely articulate young professional novelists just out of the university who write one interesting novel; well written in anyone else's way of writing; fresh because it has youth; and successful for any of the above reasons—then to be followed by other novels, demanded by the success of the first and because the author is a professional writer, and all the time the author never living any life or learning anything or seeing anything because he, or even more possibly she, is so busy writing novels.

You can study how this works out in England.

Note, *A Bibliography of the Works of Ernest Hemingway* by Louis Henry Cohn (New York: Random House, 1931), fold-out frontispiece.

Louis Henry Cohn, a New York rare-book dealer, was a captain in World War I and retained the rank thereafter. He compiled the first Hemingway bibliography.

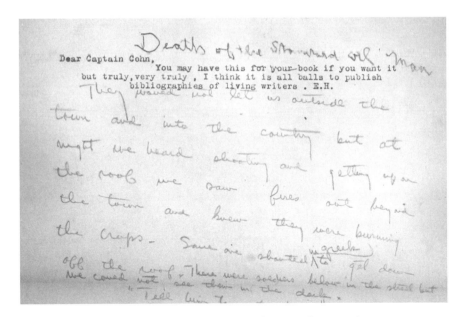

Location: Speiser and Easterling-Hallman Foundation Collection of Ernest Hemingway, Thomas Cooper Library, University of South Carolina.

Blurb on front cover of *Time for Laughter* by Robert Whitcomb (New York: Whitcomb, 1931). Location: University of Delaware Library.

Nothing is known about Hemingway's connection with Whitcomb, who published a second book, Talk United States! *with Smith and Haas in 1935.*

I was sore I had to read it but I was glad I did. . . .
You will be a damned good writer. . . .

Endorsement for *Summer Is Ended* by John Herrmann (New York: Covici-Friede, 1932), in *Contact* 1 (October 1932): 4. Location: Harry Ransom Humanities Research Center, University of Texas, Austin.

SUMMER IS ENDED
By
JOHN HERRMANN
The first novel in four years by the author of "What Happens" and the co-winner of the Scribner's Magazine short novel contest.

"John Herrmann writes of the tragedy of the human heart as truly as any writer that ever lived."

Ernest Hemingway.

$2.00 Everywhere

COVICI-FRIEDE, PUBLISHERS

Blurb on dust-jacket band and front flap of *Conquistador* by Archibald MacLeish (Boston: Houghton Mifflin, 1932). Location (without band): Collection of Matthew J. and Arlyn Bruccoli.

MacLeish (1892–1982) and Hemingway were close friends in France during the Twenties; Hemingway dedicated Winner Take Nothing *(1933) to him.*

If it is of any interest to you to read great poetry as it is published, before it becomes classic and compulsory, I advise you to read "Conquistador."

Letter to *Hound and Horn* 6 (October–December 1932): 135. Location: Matthew J. and Arlyn Bruccoli Collection of F. Scott Fitzgerald of F. Scott Fitzgerald, Thomas Cooper Library, University of South Carolina.

Lawrence Leighton's "An Autopsy and a Prescription," Hound and Horn *5 (July–September 1932): 520–39, stated: "I wish to consider the work of Messrs. Ernest Hemingway, John Dos Passos, and F. Scott Fitzgerald and to indicate my reasons for finding it repulsive, sterile, and dead. Also I wish by examining the work of their contemporary, the late Raymond Radiguet, to suggest qualities the cultivation of which would render American fiction more interesting than it is now." Hemingway's response refers to the homosexual relationship between Radiguet and Jean Cocteau. Leighton was an instructor at Dartmouth College.*

To the Editors,
The Hound and Horn.
Sirs:

Referring to Mr. Lawrence Leighton's very interesting and revealing autopsy on Mr. Dos Passos, Mr. Fitzgerald and myself, may I take exception to one sentence:

"One feels behind Radiguet, Mme. de Lafayette, Benjamin Constant, Proust, even Racine."

Surely this should read "Radiguet behind Mme. de Lafayette." The rest of the sentence might stand although it would be more just to place Cocteau behind Radiguet and give Racine the benefit of the doubt. But perhaps Mr. Leighton has a feeling for Racine and would not wish to deprive him of his place.

Yours very truly,
Ernest Hemingway

Cooke, Montana,
August 27, 1932.

Letter to Robert M. Coates, *The New Yorker* 8 (5 November 1932): 74.

Coates (1897–1973) had known Hemingway in Paris during the Twenties. He wrote The Eater of Darkness *(1926), which has been described by Malcolm Cowley as the first American Dada novel. In 1926 Coates began a thirty-year career as a critic for* The New Yorker.

My friend Ernest Hemingway has objected to one of my remarks about "Death in the Afternoon." In my review, I said that "there are passages in which his bitterness descends to petulance (as in his gibes at William Faulkner . . . T. S. Eliot, Aldous Huxley, Jean Cocteau . . .)."[1] Such was my impression on reading the book, but such, at least in the case of William Faulkner, was not Hemingway's intention, as will appear from the following letter, which I print here with his permission, on the understanding that it appear in full:

Cooke, Montana
October 5
Dear Bob:
There weren't any cracks against Faulkner. You read it over and you will see. Your interpretations, opinions and judgements are naturally none of my goddamned business-es, and would not comment on them—this only as question of fact. There was a mention, a pretty damned friendly mention. There was a crack at Cocteau (who is a public character and perfectly crack-able), there was re-buttal to W. Frank, Eliot and Huxley.

The Eliot thing has been back and forth for a long time. Frank is a twirp (pen in hand), no matter how admirable politically. Huxley is a smart fellow, a very smart fellow.

I don't really think of you as a critic—no disparagement, I mean I think of you as a writer—or would not make any explanations. Certainly, books should be judged by those who read them—not explained by the writer.

But I'm damned if I wrote any petulant jibes against Faulkner and the hell with you telling citizens that I did.

All the petulant jibes you like against Waldo Frank (or yourself even, if you're looking for them), or anyone for whom I have no particular respect. But I have plenty of respect for Faulkner and wish him all luck. That does not mean that I would not joke about him. There are no subjects that I would not jest about if the jest were funny enough (just as, liking wing shooting, I would shoot my own mother if she went in coveys and had a good strong flight). If it was not funny to you that is my, or perhaps your, hard luck.

Always,
Your friend,
Ernest Hemingway

1. 1 October 1932, 61–62.

Letter to the *New Republic* (1933), in *Great Companions* by Max Eastman (New York: Farrar, Straus and Cudahy, 1959), 57. Location: Speiser and Easterling-Hallman Foundation Collection of Ernest Hemingway, Thomas Cooper Library, University of South Carolina.

Hemingway's letter (not printed by the New Republic) *responded to East-man's review of* Death in the Afternoon *("Bull in the Afternoon," New Republic 75 [7 June 1933]: 94–97), which referred to Hemingway's "literary style, you might say, of wearing false hair on the chest." Hemingway inter-preted this comment as an insinuation that he was impotent. A well-publicized scuffle resulted when he encountered Eastman in Maxwell Perkins's office at Charles Scribner's Sons in August 1937.*

Sirs:

Would it not be possible for you to have Mr. Max Eastman elaborate his nostalgic speculations on my sexual incapacity? Here they would be read (aloud) with much enjoyment (our amusements are simple) and I should be glad to furnish illustrations to brighten up Mr. Eastman's prose if you consid-ered them advisable. Mr. Alexander Woolcott and the middle-aged Mr. East-man having both published hopeful doubts as to my potency is it too much to expect that we might hear soon from Mr. Stark Young?[1]

Yours etc. . . .

Ernest Hemingway

1. Woollcott was impotent; Young was a homosexual.

Blurb on front dust jacket of *My Life and Hard Times* by James Thurber (New York: Harper, 1933).

Thurber (1894–1961) and Hemingway were friends; the blurb includes a dig at Gertrude Stein's The Autobiography of Alice B. Toklas *(1933), which belittled Hemingway.*

By the author of "THE SEAL IN THE BEDROOM"

My Life and Hard Times
By James Thurber
With Illustrations by **The Author**

Ernest Hemingway says: "I find it far superior to the autobiography of Henry Adams. Even in the earliest days when Thurber was writing under the name of Alice B. Toklas we knew he had it in him if he could get it out."

HARPER & BROTHERS - ESTABLISHED 1817

Location: Lilly Library, Indiana University.

Statement on Ezra Pound, *The Cantos of Ezra Pound: Some Testimonies* (New York: Farrar & Rinehart, 1933), 13. Location: Beinecke Library, Yale University.

Other contributors to this booklet included Ford Madox Ford, T. S. Eliot, Hugh Walpole, Archibald MacLeish, H.D. (Hilda Doolittle), and James Joyce.

Any poet born in this century or in the last ten years of the preceding century who can honestly say that he has not been influenced by or learned greatly from the work of Ezra Pound deserves to be pitied rather than rebuked. It is as if a prose writer born in that time should not have learned from or been influenced by James Joyce or that a traveller should pass through a great blizzard and not have felt its cold or a sand storm and not have felt the sand and the wind. The best of Pound's writing—and it is in the CANTOS—will last as long as there is any literature.

 21 Nov. 1932

Blurb on dust jacket for *A Draft of X X X Cantos* by Ezra Pound (New York: Farrar & Rinehart, 1933), dust jacket.

Of the statements provided by the authors who contributed to the booklet that accompanied A Draft of X X X Cantos, *only Hemingway's was excerpted as a cover endorsement.*

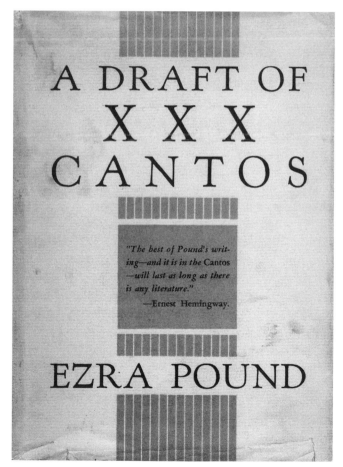

Location: Lilly Library, Indiana University.

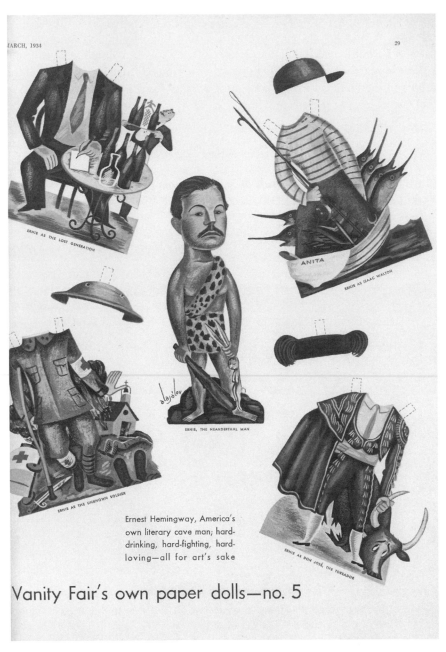

ERNIE AS THE LOST GENERATION

ANITA

ERNIE AS ISAAC WALTON

ERNIE, THE NEANDERTHAL MAN

ERNIE AS THE UNKNOWN SOLDIER

Ernest Hemingway, America's
own literary cave man; hard-
drinking, hard-fighting, hard-
loving—all for art's sake

ERNIE AS DON JOSÉ, THE TOREADOR

Vanity Fair's own paper dolls—no. 5

Alajàlov's *Vanity Fair* caricature of Hemingway. *Vanity Fair*, 42 (March 1934): 29.
Location: Speiser and Easterling-Hallman Foundation Collection of Ernest
Hemingway, Thomas Cooper Library, University of South Carolina.

Introduction, *This Must Be the Place* by Jimmie the Barman (James Charters), ed. Morrill Cody (London: Herbert Joseph, 1934). Location: Matthew J. and Arlyn Bruccoli Collection of F. Scott Fitzgerald, Thomas Cooper Library, University of South Carolina.

Englishman Charters (1897–1975), a former boxer, was a well-liked barman at the Dingo, the Falstaff, and other Montparnasse cafes. Hemingway's introduction begins with a sneer directed at Gertrude Stein's The Autobiography of Alice B. Toklas *(1933).*

Once a woman has opened a salon it is certain that she will write her memoirs. If you go to the salon you will be in the memoirs; that is, you will be if your name ever becomes known enough so that its use, or abuse, will help the sale of the woman's book. Even if your name means nothing to those strange folk who pay cash for literary reminiscences (I understand they have been banded into clubs or guilds, perhaps for their own protection) you will still have your place in the memoirs if you will devote yourself loyally enough and long enough to serving the cause of the woman and of her salon, and, quite too often, of her art. Such women usually write, but they have been known to practise sculpture and to paint as well. But if you are mentioned only for loyalty to the establishment and for services rendered, you must not expect a very lengthy citation.

The best way to achieve an at all exhaustive mention (outside of having the salon woman purchase your sculpture, your paintings, your wash drawings, or perhaps your embroidered diapers, if embroidering is your art, while these objects are still very cheap and continue to hold them after they become expensive, so that mention of them would be calculated to increase their value) is to have the woman be fond of you and then get over it. The reasons for the getting over it may be many: you may be no longer so young; you may lose your teeth, your hair, your disposition, your money, your shoes, your shirts may not come back from the laundry; anything in fact. Or you may get very tired of seeing the woman or of hearing her talk. It may be that the getting over it is induced by domestic compulsion, or by the changes of the seasons, or it may be anything you say, but the memoir writer will usually prove that a lady's brain may still be between her thighs, even though those thighs—but let us not make jokes about thighs—and will treat you in her memoirs exactly as any girl around the Dôme or the Select would, imputing you this, denying you that, and only withholding the Billingsgate because it would fit illy in the pantheon to her own glory that every self-made legendary woman hopes to erect with her memoirs.

That is how to achieve a lengthy mention, if you want one. But you must start young. Literary ladies like them young or famous; and not too famous and famous in some other line. Literary salon women do not like Mr. James Joyce, for instance. They would be happier if there had not been any Mr. James Joyce. However, if you go to the salon you must expect to be in the memoirs.

Now a saloon, or bar, is different. You should expect to be able to go into a saloon or bar and pay for your drinks without appearing in the bartender's memoirs, and I was shocked and grieved to hear that Jimmy Charters was writing his. It is only a step from abolishing the right of sanctuary in the Republic of San Marion to permitting bartenders to write their memoirs, and surely Jimmy served more and better drinks than any legendary woman ever did in her salon. Certainly Jimmy gave less and better advice; I can hear him saying, "You should go home, sir. Shall I get a taxi?" and if he wants to write his memoirs it is only one more step in the decline of Western civilization. Besides, I am very fond of Jimmy. He was always charming and he was, and is, an excellent barman. Like everyone in Montparnasse, the most interesting part of his life was before he crossed to the left bank of the Seine, but, like almost everyone else there, he did not realize that. If his book has only one half of his charm, one quarter of his knowledge, and one quarter of his experience, it should still be a fairly intoxicating volume. I wish it were not about Montparnasse, because that is a dismal place. But Jimmy could make it very cheerful when he was behind the bar. Here's luck to him putting it in a book.

SERENGETTI PLAINS,

TANGANYIKA.

December, 1933.

"The Farm," *Cahiers d'Art* 9, nos. 1–4 (1934): 28–29. Location: Museum of Modern Art.

"The Farm" is not about Miró's painting: it is about Hemingway's love of art. The statement includes another attack on Gertrude Stein's writing and lesbianism.

When I first knew Miró he had very little money and very little to eat and he worked all day every day for nine months painting a very large and wonderful picture called "The Farm." He did not want to sell this picture nor even to have it away from him. No one could look at it and not know it had been painted by a great painter and when you are painting things that people must take on trust it is good to have something around that has taken as long to make as it takes a woman to make a child (a woman who isn't a woman can

The Farm. Location: National Gallery of Art, Washington, D.C. Gift of Mary Hemingway.

usually write her autobiography in a third of that time) and that shows even fools that you are a great painter in terms that they understand.

After Miró had painted "The Farm" and after James Joyce had written *Ulysses* they had a right to expect people to trust the further things they did even when the people did not understand them and they have both kept on working very hard.

If you have painted "The Farm" or if you have written *Ulysses,* and then keep on working very hard afterwards, you do not need an Alice B. Toklas.

Finally everyone had to sell everything and if Miró was to have a dealer he had to let "The Farm" go with the other pictures. But Shipman,[1] who found him the dealer, made the dealer put a price on it and agree to sell it to him. This was probably the only good business move that Shipman ever did in his life. But doing a good business move must have made him uncomfortable because he came to me the same day and said, "Hem, you should have *The Farm.* I do not love anything as much as you care for that picture and you ought to have it."

I argued against this explaining to him that it was not only how much I cared about it. There was the value to consider.

"It is going to be worth much more than we will ever have, Evan. You have no idea what it will be worth," I told him.

"I don't care about that," he said. "If it's money I'll shoot you dice for it. Let the dice decide about the money. You'll never sell it anyway."

"I have no right to shoot. You're shooting against yourself."

"Let the dice decide the money," Shipman insisted. "If I lose it will be mine. Let the dice show."

So we rolled dice and I won and made the first payment. We agreed to pay five thousand francs for *The Farm* and that was four thousand two hundred and fifty francs more than I had ever paid for a picture. The picture naturally stayed with the dealer.

When it was time to make the last payment the dealer came around and was very pleased because there was no money in the house or in the bank. If we did not pay the money that day he kept the picture. Dos Passos, Shipman and I finally borrowed the money around various bars and restaurants, got the picture and brought it home in a taxi. The dealer felt very bad because he had already been offered four times what we were paying. But we explained to him as it is so often explained to you in France, that business is business.

In the open taxi the wind caught the big canvas as though it were a sail and we made the taxi driver crawl along. At home we hung it and everyone looked at it and was very happy. I would not trade it for any picture in the world. Miró came and looked at it and said, "I am very content that you have *The Farm*."

When I see him now he says, "I am always content, *tu sais*, that you have *The Farm*."

It has in it all that you feel about Spain when you are there and all that you feel when you are away and cannot go there. No one else has been able to paint these two very opposing things. Although Juan Gris painted it how it is when you know that you will never go there. Picasso is very different. Picasso is a business man. So were some of the greatest painters that ever lived. But this is too long now and the thing to do is look at the picture, not write about it.

1. Evan Shipman (1904–57), minor poet and horse-racing fancier, was a lifelong friend of Hemingway's.

Introduction to *Quintanilla* (New York: Pierre Matisse Gallery, [1934];
Philadelphia: Boyer Galleries, [1934]). Location for both: Speiser and
Easterling-Hallman Foundation Collection of Ernest Hemingway, Thomas
Cooper Library, University of South Carolina.

*Luis Quintanilla (1893–1978) was a Spanish revolutionist; Hemingway's
introduction to an exhibition of his engravings denounces phony liberals. The
sixth paragraph describes the activities of real revolutionists, conveying the
impression that Hemingway had done these things.*

If this exposition of dry points by Luis Quintanilla had been two months
ago, the list of patrons would have been headed by His Excellency the Spanish Ambassador, His Excellency the American Ambassador to Spain and followed by other dignitaries and names of people.

As it is there are no patrons, the artist is in jail in Madrid charged with
being a member of the revolutionary committee of the October revolt in Spain
with the prosecuting attorney asking a sentence of sixteen years of hard labor
for him, and the only excellencies are in these magnificent etchings.

Good Spanish painters are always in trouble. It is a country where the tradition is, and it may be a foolish tradition, I will not argue it with you, that a
man should be a man as well as an artist. Velazquez, with the least brains and
no ambition but to paint and be respectable, had servant trouble. He tried to
be, too well, the perfect servant of royalty and it killed him, finally. Goya's trou-
bles came, mostly, from what he carried between his thighs and they were
fairly continuous, very interesting to study, and sometimes seem unnecessary.
But the necessary misfortunes we never make ourselves.

If we omit the Greek who, not being a Spaniard, cannot be judged by his
trouble, which was religion, there are no other really good ones until Picasso
and Juan Gris. Picasso has been in grave trouble for a number of years now
through money and the desire for money. Juan Gris died in great trouble over
the self-imposed lack of it. Miro's trouble is quite complicated yet very simple
and he could do with a little more of it, and now here is Quintanilla in trouble with revolution.

On the day, a not dull day, that I had a cable in Havana from two friends in
Madrid saying in a clearly decipherable yet mystifying to a censor, impromptu
code, "Luis hoosegowed," signed Ziff Allen, I received, forwarded in the mail,
a mimeographed sheet entitled, The Event of the Year, which event was a literary tea to be given at the studio of someone for the guest pickets of the
Macaulay Company. The invitation to be present, to picket and to proceed to
the self-styled literary tea was signed by a man who, since two years, cannot
write fifty consecutive words without using the word revolution.

Now this may possibly be a good time to suggest that a small tax be levied on the use of the word revolution, the proceeds to be given to the defence of, say, such people as Luis Quintanilla, or any of your friends who are in jail, by all those who write the word and never have shot nor been shot at; who never have stored arms nor filled a bomb, nor have discovered arms nor had a bomb burst among them; who never have gone hungry in a general strike, nor have manned streetcars when the tracks are dynamited; who never have sought cover in a street trying to get their heads behind a gutter; who never have seen a woman shot in the head, in the breast or in the buttocks; who never have seen an old man with the top of his head off; who never have walked with their hands up; who never have shot a horse or seen hooves smash a head; who never have sat a horse and been shot at or stoned; who never have been cracked on the head with a club nor have thrown a brick; who never have seen a scab's forearms broken with a crow-bar, or an agitator filled up with compressed air with an air hose; who, now it gets more serious—that is, the penalty is more severe—have never moved a load of arms at night in a big city; nor standing, seeing it moved, knowing what it was and afraid to denounce it because they did not want to die later; nor (let's end it, it could go on too long) stood on a roof trying to urinate on their hands to wash off the black in the fork between finger and thumb from the back-spit of a Thompson gun, the gun thrown in a cistern and the troops coming up the stairs; the hands are what they judge you by—the hands are all the evidence they need although they won't acquit you on them being clean if they are sure of the roof; nor even come up with the troops.

No. The word revolution should be taxed, and guest pickets if they wish to speak it at the Event of the Year, should wear a celluloid badge, something like a hunting license, showing they have paid for the privilege.

Luis Quintanilla, who has the right to use that word, is very sparing of it. He does not take the money and rant to save his soul like Diego Rivera. He has painted great frescoes in the Casa del Pueblo and the Ciudad Universitario in Madrid and there are no symbols of capitalism, or any symbols in them. Always there are people as there are people in the etchings. He does not judge them; only presents them because he has led them in action. If you follow you idealize. If you have led you present and criticize, you have the right to satirize, and when you hate, you hate intelligently.

Quintanilla in whose apartment the arms were stored when it was not known that it would be a bloodless revolution that sent out Alfonso, Quintanilla who raised the republican flag over the royal palace, climbing up and running it up with his own hands before it was certain there was an abdication, and who took no credit and never let it be referred to without joking, where

QUINTANILLA

BOYER GALLERIES INC
BROAD STREET STATION BUILDING
PHILADELPHIA PENNA
DECEMBER 10 TO DECEMBER 24

The exhibition opened at the Pierre Matisse Gallery in New York and was subsequently transferred to the Boyer Galleries.

he would have been embalmed in school books if it had been an American revolution; this Quintanilla draws with a sharp instrument on nickled zinc to make etchings that are beautiful and lasting in any epoch at any time; etchings that can speak familiarly with thee and thou, without affectation of comradeship, by merit, with any etcher that has ever lived. And I believe that those who use the word revolution easily, too easily, to save their souls or to make a career, should pay a small tax to those who have a right to shout it as they were supposed to shout and sound horns in the north of that country a long time ago.

But those who truly have a right to use that word, through exposition of their bodies and their liberty, speak very quietly, do their other work (and all good work goes to the same end) well; and when they are in jail write that they are quite comfortable, with good people, not at all discouraged, ask how you are and how are all the children, naming them, and is the hunting season good, better than this time last year when we were in Extremadura after wild boar (he wrote before that in November and December he would be in Holland, very good pictures there and in Belgium on the way) but he is very well in jail and will I write and tell him all the news, really in jail it is very funny.

So there, like a moving cloud, comes the shadow of sixteen years of a fine artist's life (from thirty-nine to fifty-five that makes) that the state asks to take away. So here are the etchings. Take a good look at them. It is your luck to see them, and to have them, because the man who made them might as well have been in jail or killed two years ago when they put the Bourbon out. But that was a good one, that one succeeded. So a man had time to work, to make this world, and scratch it on nickled zinc a line at a time, a million lines, that make a world where there is light and depth and space, humor, pity and understanding, and a sound earthy knowledge that gives us the first true Madrid that we have seen since Goya.

Now he is in jail and the great frescoes he was making for the monument to Pablo Igleseas will not be completed. This last revolution it seems was a bad one; not like the good one that brought honor and the chance to work. A good one, you know, is one that succeeds. A bad one is one that fails.

You who read the catalogue are all right, you know. You must not feel badly. Do not let it disturb you. Madrid is a long way away and you never heard of this man before. What did he get in trouble for anyway?

Sure. That is the way to look at it. But look at the etchings. Take a good look at the etchings.

Mimeographed appeal to the President of the Spanish Republic on behalf of Luis Quintanilla (1934).

The release of Quintanilla, who was arrested in October 1934 for antigovernment activities, became the object of an international campaign, led in the United States by Hemingway and John Dos Passos. Although the protests and petitions were ignored by Spanish officials, Quintanilla was released on 10 June 1935. He left Spain in January 1939 for exile in the United States.

```
To His Excellency Senor Don Niceto Alcala Zamora,
The President of the Spanish Republic,
Palacio Nacional, Madrid.


Your Excellency:

          Among the prisoners held as a result of
the events of October, 1934, is the painter Luis
Quintanilla, in our opinion a great Spanish etcher
who continues a great tradition, who is also a
painter of great ability. Without presuming to form
an opinion on the merits of the situation, with
which  we as foreigners have no concern, we, the
undersigned, should like to point out to your excellency
and to the members of the Spanish government, that
great artistic ability and the long training of
the skill of the eye and hand that is needed to make
a great artist and to produce valuable and authentic
works of art, is a rare thing in any nation or
generation, and that during all the bloody ages of
European political and party strife has been admitted
by the cultured world to be a rare thing and even the
chief glory of a nation or a generation.

          We, the undersigned, considering the
etchings of Luis Quintanilla one of the most
important artistic documents of the present generation
of Spaniards, speaking as old admirers of the
artistic and intellectual greatness of the Spanish
nation, would like to bring the situation of
Luis Quintanilla to the attention of his excellency
the President of the Republic and the members of the
government and to ask them to keep these things in
mind when dealing with the case of a man whose work,
although he is still young and perhaps some of the
best of it is still unknown outside of the artistic
circles, already redounds greatly to the credit of
the fatherland of Goya and Velasquez.


This petition was signed by the following persons:-

   Leopold Stokowski
   Jascha Heifetz
   Efrem Zimbalist
   John Carroll
   Fritz Reiner
   Sinclair Lewis
   Theodore Dreiser
   Waldo Pierce
   Ernest Hemingway
   John Dos Passos
```

Location: Speiser and Easterling-Hallman Foundation Collection of Ernest Hemingway, Thomas Cooper Library, University of South Carolina.

Introduction, *Gattorno* (Havana: Ucar, Garcia y Cia, 1935).

These comments on Antonio Gattorno (1904–80) employ Hemingway's simple-pretentious style: "every artist owes it to the place he knows best to either destroy it or perpetuate it" and "Gattorno can be much better than he is although he can never be any better than he is at the time."

Gattorno is a cuban painter who is also a painter for the world. He was fortunate to be born in Cuba so that he could leave it and having left it he had the good sense to return to it to paint. Now it is time for him to leave it again but he will always return to it wherever he is painting.

When he first went to Europe he was sixteen years old and had already won a scholarship from the Academy of Painting of San Alejandro de la Habana. He must have been a very strange wonder-child then, because he is now at thirty-one the youngest person that I know although there is no youth in his painting. Neither is there any age. There is simply good painting which, when it is good enough, is always ageless. But it can be more important if the painter knows the painting that is behind all good painting and the line of descent that all good painting has followed. Gattorno had the luck to go to Italy as a barbarian at a time in his life when the primitives seemed to be painted by his contemporaries. He had never met any contemporaries of his own and in Italy he saw good painting and grew up with it feeling that these were the painters that were his friends and that he could call them all tu and toi. It was a strange thing that they had all been dead for many centuries but that is the way it is in painting when you are born to be a good painter.

He went to Spain but people have, always, to take a choice between Italy and Spain and since he had gone first to Italy and because he is tormented by loyalties he could not abandon Italy so he did not get much from Spain. Then, too, Spain was shocking to him. Spain is an open wound on the right arm that cannot heal because the dust gets in it, while Cuba is a beautiful ulcer somewhere else. Of course, too, he could not speak Spanish. He speaks Cuban. And Cubans do not like Spaniards while every-one when they are sixteen like Italians. But he found Galicia very sad. He is quite proud of this because it makes him feel like an intellectual and like all people who are not intellectual he is very proud when he is that way.

Then he went on to Paris and there it was the same as in Italy. He understood and saw all about modern painting and it was all quite natural to him. They were his contemporaries too although the only one who was dead, by then, was Modigliani. There is no mystery when you are part of the mystery. Gattorno painted very well in Paris.

Back in Cuba he saw it all now as a painter and, like the greatest ones, each time he painted a picture he tried to get all of it in; no matter what the size of the picture nor whether it had only two figures in it he tried to put all Cuba in it. He did not paint buck niggers, nor rumbas, because he had no desire to interfere with the province of music. He painted the people of the long, sad, overfoliaged island with the skill and knowledge of a painter who could have become a great abstractionist and he made some marvellous pictures. In the pictures is his delicacy, his aloof passion, his detachment and his full understanding. Then it was over; because Cuba is even more a place to leave than a place to return to.

Why is it a place to leave?

Because a painter cannot make his living there, because he can never see any great painting to wash his mind clear and encourage his heart, because if he gets to be a great painter no one would ever know it nor would they buy enough of his paintings for him to be able to eat. There is no one there even who can photograph a painting properly and no one to reproduce it as it should be reproduced.

Why is it a place to come back to?

Because you are born there and every artist owes it to the place he knows best to either destroy it or perpetuate it.

Now he must work. He does not know how much he must work because he can see that it is all in a single picture when he paints that picture. But to live you must, if not repeat, insist. He must go on insisting. He will never be bankrupt because you cannot bankrupt pure skill. And no one owes anything to the world. But I would like to see him paint much more because while he can put it all in one picture he can put it all in again and there will be other things. It is like hauling through the same part of the sea with a net with different dimensions of mesh. But if he will not change his net and wants to go to other seas why then let him go. And when he returns again there will be other fish in these waters that will not go through his mesh.

The thing for him to do is to paint, wherever he is. But to do that he has to eat, to buy his materials and to have a place to work. As things are organized now he could risk his hide a few times for one party or another and if that party won, and had the loot at its disposal, he could get his share in an official appointment. But to see Gattorno, who was made for painting and for nothing else, and to ask him to fight is as sensible, economically and tactically, as to use a camel's hair brush from a bayonet. So he has to go.

The trouble with people who do things perfectly as they go along is that they do not realize that they improve. Gattorno can be much better than he is although he can never be any better than he is at the time. He must go on and he must paint.

Antonio Gattorno was born March 15, 1904, in La Habana. He is a Cuban and has lived all his life in Cuba, except for seven years spent studying and travelling in Italy, Spain, France, Belgium and Germany. For the last three years he has lived and worked in the suburb of Marianao of La Habana.

Location: Speiser and Easterling-Hallman Foundation Collection of Ernest Hemingway, Thomas Cooper Library, University of South Carolina.

Letter, *American Big Game Fishing* by Mrs. Oliver C. Grinnell, Frances H. Low, Herman P. Gray, Charles L. Lehmann, Lynn Bogue Hunt, Ernest Hemingway, Van Campen Heilner, George C. Thomas III, David M. Newell, Otto J. Scheer, Francis H. Geer, S. Kip Farrington Jr., Thomas G. F. Aitken, and Eugene V. Connett (New York: Derrydale Press, 1935), 49–51. Location: Speiser and Easterling-Hallman Foundation Collection of Ernest Hemingway, Thomas Cooper Library, University of South Carolina.

Hemingway developed his enthusiasm for saltwater fishing after he took up residence in Key West. In 1934 he purchased his thirty-eight-foot sport-fishing boat, The Pilar, *and became an authority on game fishing.*

The largest sailfish ever taken in the Atlantic was caught in the spring of 1934. This is an extraordinary sail for these waters and it is a record that will probably never be beaten. The following extract from a letter about the fish from Ernest Hemingway to the author tells the story in graphic Hemingway manner.

"The big sailfish was caught on May 23, 1934, about 8 miles from Key West on what is called the 10 fathom bar just off the Western Dry Rocks. Thomas J. S. McGrath was fishing with me and we left the docks at 2:30 P.M. Inside of an hour he was hooked into a good sailfish on light tackle which a shark took from him after about forty-five minutes and fifteen jumps. I had an amberjack and grouper outfit 16 oz. Hardy tip, old style Pflueger Templar reel and 21 thread baited, and as I was handling the boat, etc. myself told him to slack this out while we put on another bait. The big sailfish smashed the bait almost as soon as it was out. McGrath shouted for me to take him, that his arm was still cramped from the other fish and that he couldn't deal with him. I told him to stay with him, that I would handle the boat for him and that he would find his arm would clear up. But his arm was really bad and after a few minutes he insisted that I take the fish. He had been ill with arthritis and was in no condition to fish or would certainly have caught the fish. I took the fish over with no idea how big he was and was amazed at how he could pull. I promptly announced that he was foul hooked because no sailfish could pull that hard on 21 thread line. I treated him as though he were foul hooked and worked him very hard, standing up with him out on the stern. Brought him to gaff pretty quickly, saw how big he was, told the amateur gaffer to gaff him in the head; he pricked him somewhere toward the tail and we had fireworks. There was nobody to handle the wheel who had ever been on the boat before and I had less than two hundred yards of line. Fought him on the spring of }the rod like a salmon with the lever drag off (you know how that old style Templar works) using my fingers for the braking. Was afraid to let him get out far for fear he would make a run and pop the line. Holding him close and bringing him up to easy gaffing six times with the citizen missing him each time, passed the rod, reel and all under the stern, under the propeller and rudder each time he went under the boat. He finally gaffed him and we took him on board 43 minutes after he was hooked. At no time, after I took him over, did he have more than sixty yards out. Most of the time he was about twenty yards out; but strong. He pulled like an amberjack; jumped clear eleven times. We weighed him on a tested scale before eight witnesses including Charles P. Thompson of this city, Darrell Lowe, Al Dudek, and others and he was 119 ½ pounds. With a steel tape measured 9 feet ¾ inch and girth 35 inches. Thomas J. S. McGrath of Shreveport, La., has all the measurements, length of bill, etc. The fish has been mounted and is in Key West for anybody to see. I would of course not send him in as a record since I did not hook him and McGrath would not because he did not land him. It was a female fish and was very beautifully built. Was caught on a flood tide around four-thirty in the afternoon in ten fathoms of water with a heavy, dark stream on strip mullet bait."

Hemingway celebrating his catch in Key West in the mid-1930s. Matador Sidney Franklin (in beret) is to the right of the fish. Location: Hemingway Collection, John F. Kennedy Library.

Letter, "Hemingway on Mutilated Fish," *Outdoor Life* 77 (June 1936): 70–72.

So many deep-sea anglers, in returning the questionnaire I sent them to learn their stand on mutilated fish, wrote letters that it was possible to include only excerpts in my article last month. One letter, though was so full of meat and discussed the problem of records so thoroughly that, rather than lose any of it, I held it over. It is given here in its entirety. It comes from Ernest Hemingway, novelist and noted big game angler. This interesting and thought-provoking letter begins immediately below.—T. A. [Thomas Aitken, editor of the "Big Game Fishing" column]

I believe rod-and-reel records should be of two classes—those that show the largest fish caught on rod and reel—regardless of whether the angler had assistance or not—and those in which no one touched the rod or the line from the time the angler hooked the fish until the leader was in the boatman's hands. In this way the first records show the size of fish which can be taken on rod and reel; the second show the prowess of the individual angler.

A case in point is the 119½-lb. Atlantic sailfish which was hooked and fought for a few minutes by T. J. S. McGrath, and then fought and landed by me. Neither McGrath nor I would enter this fish as a record for ourselves since neither of us hooked, fought, or landed the fish without assistance. But the unusual size of the fish for the Atlantic Ocean is certainly worthy of record. It is the largest sailfish, to date, caught in the Atlantic, but neither angler can claim it as a record. McGrath had an arm crippled with arthritis and, while an enthusiastic fisherman, did not want to hook into a big fish because of his condition. In spite of this, he had just hooked and lost a sailfish that a shark attacked after the fish had made 14 jumps. He had just slacked out a line to hold it, while I prepared another bait, when the big sailfish struck. His arm was so crippled from the work on the previous fish that he turned the big fish over to me to fight, under my protest. Now, neither of us would claim the fish as a record, but the fact remains that it is the largest caught on rod and reel in the Atlantic, and should be so listed, together with the fact that it was hooked by one man and fought and landed by another.

I understand that very large tuna have been taken on rod and reel after the fish have been fought by several different people. If these fish are larger than any other that has been caught on rod and reel, why not list them, asking the men who caught them to give their weight and measurements and the names of the various people who handled the rods, and exact details of the catch? Such fish would be listed in the records for size of fish, rather than in those in which the angler received no assistance.

I have frequently seen fish lost or eaten by sharks through the utter exhaustion of the angler. If the man who hooks a fish turns the rod over to another angler, he should so state when reporting the capture of the fish, and, if the fish is larger than any other ever caught by rod and reel, it should be recorded in a separate list with the names of the men who fought it. If the fish were hand-lined, or harpooned, or shot, it should not be listed as caught by rod and reel, but, if it is of extraordinary size, would come under the list of fish taken by any means, such as commercial fishing, nets, harpooning, etc.

In that way there would be three just classifications of record fish:

First—Size and weight of fish taken by any means. Useful to science and to the fisherman as showing to what size his quarry are known to grow. This has nothing to do with sportsmanship.

Second—Size and weight of the largest fish taken on rod and reel as the catch of any individual angler, if the fish were disqualified because another angler gave assistance, with a note in parenthesis to this effect, with the names of the men aiding in the fighting of the fish. This list would be in value to the angler as showing the size and weight of fish he could hope to capture on rod and reel by himself, without assistance, provided he had the necessary physical condition and stamina.

Third—Size and weight of largest fish taken on rod and reel by individual anglers without assistance in the hooking or fighting of the fish. This list should give details of the tackle and the time taken to bring the fish to gaff.

Now about mutilation. If a fish is killed by sharks, certainly the angler should not receive credit for killing him. But, if a fish is attacked by sharks after he is gaffed or when the fish is whipped by the angler and the boatman is holding the leader, I believe the angler should receive full credit for catching him as he will be penalized in the recording of the fish by the blood and weight lost.

Take this instance: Say three men are fishing in a launch off the north coast of Cuba. There is the angler, the man at the wheel, and the mate. The day is very rough. Say the angler hooks, fights, and brings to gaff a marlin weighing 1,200 lb. As soon as the fish is gaffed, he bleeds. As soon as he bleeds, sharks show up. There will be at least 14 ft. of that fish in the water. If a shark takes a bite out of him while he is being made fast alongside is he to be disqualified as a record fish?

Who is going to do the disqualifying? If any three of the disqualifiers were there in a heavy sea such as you get off Cuba in the afternoon, do they think they could put that fish in the cockpit or guarantee to keep sharks away from him while making him fast?

Here is another practical side of the shark business. You whip a marlin completely and have him coming to the boat, his fin and tail out of water ready to gaff. A shark shows up and your fish, which has given up the fight, starts out again with the shark after him. You have a choice of letting him run free, which usually would mean having the shark hit him way out, since he is exhausted, or of rough-housing him and holding him tighter than you should, and possibly breaking him off. Say you land him either way, and the shark has hit him, perhaps once, in the first rush he made. Do you think the shark helped the angler land that fish?

What does mutilation consist of? Is any wound a mutilation, or does it imply a crippling of the fish? If you catch a fish that is so big that he has to be cut in two or three pieces to be weighed, is that mutilation?

The world's record marlin as recognized by OUTDOOR LIFE was cut into pieces to be weighed. Yet a bigger fish, which had some of his tail meat torn away while at gaff, according to the man who caught him, is not recognized.

Let us clear this up. What *is* mutilation? I would certainly recognize both of the above fish.

I take no sides in this, because I fish for fun, not for records. I can tell when I whip a fish or when he whips me. The only thing is that he has a hook in his mouth so that he can whip me several times, sometimes, and I can still bring him in. But I wish that instead of having a bitter fight about mutilated or unmutilated fish, fishermen could try to see each other's standpoint and without jealousy or bitterness, get together on a set of three different records which would mean something. If a fish has been hit by sharks when he was actually caught, let a note be made of that in the record, in parenthesis. The fisherman is going to feel like hell that his fish lost weight. Nobody is going to put in fish that are half eaten, and then dragged up out of the ocean, as records. In the first place they will not weigh enough to be records; in the second place the fish should be disqualified unless he was at the boat and whipped when the shark hit him. That's how it seems to me, anyway. But I'm speaking as an individual fisherman and not for any organization.

"Who Murdered the Vets? A First-Hand Report on the Florida Hurricane," *New Masses* 16 (17 September 1935): 9–10. Location: Speiser and Easterling-Hallman Foundation Collection of Ernest Hemingway, Thomas Cooper Library, University of South Carolina.

New Masses *was a communist party-line journal; although he was apolitical or antipolitical at the time, Hemingway became connected with* New Masses *when he contributed this report and had three subsequent appearances there. Hemingway had been involved in clean-up efforts following the early September hurricane deaths of 458 veterans who had been constructing roads in the Florida Keys.*

KEY WEST, FLA.

I have led my ragamuffins where they are peppered; there's not three of my hundred and fifty left alive, and they are for the town's end to beg during life.
Shakespeare.
Yes, and now we drown those three.

Whom did they annoy and to whom was their possible presence a political danger?

Who sent them down to the Florida Keys and left them there in hurricane months?

Who is responsible for their deaths?

The writer of this article lives a long way from Washington and would not know the answers to those questions. But he does know that wealthy people, yachtsmen, fishermen such as President Hoover and President Roosevelt, do not come to the Florida Keys in hurricane months. Hurricane months are August, September and October, and in those months you see no yachts along the Keys. You do not see them because yacht owners know there would be great danger, unescapable danger, to their property if a storm should come. For the same reason, you cannot interest any very wealthy people in fishing off the coast of Cuba in the summer when the biggest fish are there. There is a known danger to property. But veterans, especially the bonus-marching variety of veterans, are not property. They are only human beings; unsuccessful human beings, and all they have to lose is their lives. They are doing coolie labor for a top wage of $45 a month and they have been put down on the Florida Keys where they can't make trouble. It is hurricane months, sure, but if anything comes up, you can always evacuate them, can't you?

This is the way a storm comes. On Saturday evening at Key West, having finished working, you go out to the porch to have a drink and read the evening paper. The first thing you see in the paper is a storm warning. You know that work is off until it is past and you are angry and upset because you were going well.

The location of the tropical disturbance is given as east of Long Island in the Bahamas and the direction it is traveling is approximately toward Key West. You get out the September storm chart which gives the tracks and dates of forty storms of hurricane intensity during that month since 1900. And by taking the rate of movement of the storm as given in the Weather Bureau Advisory you calculate that it cannot reach us before Monday noon at the earliest. Sunday you spend making the boat as safe as you can. When they refuse to haul her out on the ways because there are too many boats ahead, you buy $52 worth of new heavy hawser and shift her to what seems the safest part of the submarine base and tie her up there. Monday you nail the shutters on the house and get everything movable inside. There are northeast storm warnings flying, and at five o'clock the wind is blowing heavily and steadily from the northeast and they have hoisted the big red flags with a black square in the middle one over the other that mean a hurricane. The wind is rising hourly and the barometer is falling. All the people of the town are nailing up their houses.

You go down to the boat and wrap the lines with canvas where they will chafe when the surge starts, and believe that she has a good chance to ride it out if it comes from any direction but the northwest where the opening of the sub-basin is; provided no other boat smashes into you and sinks you. There is a booze boat seized by the Coast Guard tied next to you and you notice her stern lines are only tied to ringbolts in the stern, and you start belly-aching about that.

"For Christ sake, you know those lousy ringbolts will pull right out of her stern and then she'll come down on us."

"If she does, you can cut her loose or sink her."

"Sure, and maybe we can't get to her, too. What's the use of letting a piece of junk like that sink a good boat?"

From the last advisory you figure we will not get it until midnight, and at ten o'clock you leave the Weather Bureau and go home to see if you can get two hours' sleep before it starts, leaving the car in front of the house because you do not trust the rickety garage, putting the barometer and a flashlight by the bed for when the electric lights go. At midnight the wind is howling, the glass is 29.55 and dropping while you watch it, and rain is coming in sheets. You dress, find the car drowned out, make your way to the boat with a flashlight with branches falling and wires going down. The flashlight shorts in the rain and the wind is now coming in heavy gusts from the northwest. The captured boat has pulled her ringbolts out, and by quick handling by Jose Rodriguez, a Spanish sailor, was swung clear before she hit us. She is now pounding against the dock.

The wind is bad and you have to crouch over to make headway against it. You figure if we get the hurricane from there you will lose the boat and you never will have enough money to get another. You feel like hell. But a little after two o'clock it backs into the west and by the law of circular storms you know the storm has passed over the Keys above us. Now the boat is well-sheltered by the sea wall and the breakwater and at five o'clock, the glass having been steady for an hour, you get back to the house. As you make your way in without a light you find a tree is down across the walk and a strange empty look in the front yard shows the big old sappodillo tree is down too. You turn in.

That's what happens when one misses you. And that is about the minimum of time you have to prepare for a hurricane; two full days. Sometimes you have longer.

But what happened on the Keys?

On Tuesday, as the storm made its way up the Gulf of Mexico, it was so wild not a boat could leave Key West and there was no communication with the Keys beyond the ferry, nor with the mainland. No one knew what the storm had done, where it had passed. No train came in and there was no news by plane. Nobody knew the horror that was on the Keys. It was not until late the next day that a boat got through to Matecumbe Key from Key West.

Now, as this is written five days after the storm, nobody knows how many are dead. The Red Cross, which has steadily played down the number, announcing first forty-six then 150, finally saying the dead would not pass 300, today lists the dead and missing as 446, but the total of veterans dead and missing alone numbers 442 and there have been seventy bodies of civilians recovered. The total of dead may well pass a thousand as many bodies were swept out to sea and never will be found.

It is not necessary to go into the deaths of the civilians and their families since they were on the Keys of their own free will; they made their living there, had property and knew the hazards involved. But the veterans had been sent there; they had no opportunity to leave, nor any protection against hurricanes; and they never had a chance for their lives.

During the war, troops and sometimes individual soldiers who incurred the displeasure of their superior officers, were sometimes sent into positions of extreme danger and kept there repeatedly until they were no longer problems. I do not believe anyone, knowingly, would send U.S. war veterans into any such positions in time of peace. But the Florida Keys, in hurricane months, in the matter of casualties recorded during the building of the Florida East Coast Railway to Key West, when nearly a thousand men were killed by hurricanes, can be classed as such a position. And ignorance has never been accepted as an excuse for murder or for manslaughter.

Who sent nearly a thousand war veterans, many of them husky, hard-working and simply out of luck, but many of them close to the border of pathological cases, to live in frame shacks on the Florida Keys in hurricane months?

Why were the men not evacuated on Sunday, or, at latest, Monday morning, when it was known there was a possibility of a hurricane striking the Keys *and evacuation was their only possible protection?*

Who advised against sending the train from Miami to evacuate the veterans until four-thirty o'clock on Monday so that it was blown off the tracks before it ever reached the lower camps?

These are questions that someone will have to answer, and answer satisfactorily, unless the clearing of Anacostia Flats is going to seem an act of kindness compared to the clearing of Upper and Lower Matecumbe.

When we reached Lower Matecumbe there were bodies floating in the ferry slip. The brush was all brown as though autumn had come to these islands where there is no autumn but only a more dangerous summer, but that was because the leaves had all been blown away. There was two feet of sand over the highest part of the island where the sea had carried it and all the heavy bridge-building machines were on their sides. The island looked like the abandoned bed of a river where the sea had swept it. The railroad embankment was gone and the men who had cowered behind it and finally, when the water came, clung to the rails, were all gone with it. You could find them face down and face up in the mangroves. The biggest bunch of the dead were in the tangled, always green but now brown, mangroves behind the tank cars and the water towers. They hung on there, in shelter, until the wind and the rising water carried them away. They didn't all let go at once but only when they could hold on no longer. Then further on you found them high in the trees where the water swept them. You found them everywhere and in the sun all of them were beginning to be too big for their blue jeans and jackets that they could never fill when they were on the bum and hungry.

I'd known a lot of them at Josie Grunt's place and around the town when they would come in for pay day, and some of them were punch drunk and some of them were smart; some had been on the bum since the Argonne almost and some had lost their jobs the year before last Christmas; some had wives and some couldn't remember; some were good guys and others put their pay checks in the Postal Savings and then came over to cadge in on the drinks when better men were drunk; some liked to fight and others liked to walk around the town; and they were all what you get after a war. But who sent them there to die?

They're better off, I can hear whoever sent them say, explaining to himself. What good were they? You can't account for accidents or acts of God. They were well-fed, well-housed, well-treated and, let us suppose, now they are well dead.

But I would like to make whoever sent them there carry just one out through the mangroves, or turn one over that lay in the sun along the fill, or tie five together so they won't float out, or smell that smell you thought you'd never smell again, with luck. But now you know there isn't any luck when rich bastards make a war. The lack of luck goes on until all who take part in it are gone.

So now you hold your nose, and you, you that put in the literary columns that you were staying in Miami to see a hurricane because you needed it in your next novel and now you were afraid you would not see one, you can go on reading the paper, and you'll get all you need for your next novel; but I would like to lead you by the seat of your well-worn-by-writing-to-the-literary-columns pants up to the bunch of mangroves where there is a woman, bloated big as a balloon and upside down and there's another face down in the brush next to her and explain to you they are two damned nice girls who ran a sandwich place and filling station and that where they are is their hard luck. And you could make a note of it for your next novel and how is your next novel coming, brother writer, comrade s—t?

But just then one of eight survivors from that camp of 187 not counting twelve who went to Miami to play ball (how's that for casualties, you guys who remember percentages?) comes along and he says, "That's my old lady. Fat, ain't she?" But that guy is nuts, now, so we can dispense with him and we have to go back and get in a boat before we can check up on Camp Five.

Camp Five was where eight survived out of 187, but we only find seventy-seven of those plus two more along the fill makes sixty-nine. But all the rest are in the mangroves. It doesn't take a bird dog to locate them. On the other hand, there are no buzzards. Absolutely no buzzards. How's that? Would you believe it? The wind killed all the buzzards and all the big winged birds like pelicans too. You can find them in the grass that's washed along the fill. Hey, there's another one. He's got low shoes, put him down, man, looks about sixty, low shoes, copper-riveted overalls, blue percale shirt without collar, storm jacket, by Jesus that's the thing to wear, nothing in his pockets. Turn him over. Face tumefied beyond recognition. Hell he don't look like a veteran. He's too old. He's got grey hair. You'll have grey hair yourself this time next week. And across his back there was a great big blister as wide as his back and all ready to burst where his storm jacket had slipped down. Turn him over again. Sure he's a veteran. I know him. What's he got low shoes on for then? Maybe he made some money shooting craps and bought them. You'd don't know that guy. You can't tell him now. I know him, he hasn't got any thumb. That's how I know him. The land crabs ate his thumb. You think you know everybody. Well you waited a long time to get sick, brother. Sixty-seven of them and you got sick at the sixty-eighth.

And so you walk the fill, where there is any fill and now it's calm and clear and blue and almost the way it is when the millionaires come down in the winter except for the sandflies, the mosquitoes and the smell of the dead that always smell the same in all countries you go to—and now they smell like that in your own country. Or is it just that dead soldiers smell the same no matter what their nationality or who sends them to die?

Who sent them down there?

I hope he reads this—and how does it feel?

He will die too, himself, perhaps even without a hurricane warning, but maybe it will be an easy death, that's the best you get, so that you do not have to hang onto something until you can't hang on, until your fingers won't hold on, and it is dark. And the wind makes a noise like a locomotive passing, with a shriek on top of that, because the wind has a scream exactly as it has in books, and then the fill goes and the high wall of water rolls you over and over and then, whatever it is, you get it and we find you, now of no importance, stinking in the mangroves.

You're dead now, brother, but who left you there in the hurricane months on the Keys where a thousand men died before you in the hurricane months when they were building the road that's now washed out?

Who left you there? And what's the punishment for manslaughter now?

Wire, "Greetings on Our Twenty-Fifth Anniversary," *New Masses* 25 (1 December 1936): 21. Location: Speiser and Easterling-Hallman Foundation Collection of Ernest Hemingway, Thomas Cooper Library, University of South Carolina.

Hemingway's statement appeared with those of Max Lerner, Ruth Suckow, Howard Brubaker, Corliss Lamont, Anna Rochester, and the Confederation of Mexican Workers.

Awfully sorry cannot send story as have been working six months on novel stop Have written nothing else stop Best luck congratulations twenty-fifth anniversary will send you a good story for the fiftieth.

∾

Letter to Georges Schreiber, *Portraits and Self-Portraits* by Schreiber (Boston: Houghton Mifflin, 1936), 57.

In this autobiographical piece Hemingway untruthfully states that he "has made his own living since he was sixteen years old." It is also untrue that he worked as a dishwasher and waiter. His self-mythologizing process was flourishing by 1936.

The author, whose portrait, drawn by a man who has never seen him, appears opposite this, is thirty-eight years old, married, the father of three sons, and has published two novels, three books of short stories, a treatise on the Spanish bull ring, a satirical novel, and an account of a hunting trip in Tanganyika. He has made his own living since he was sixteen years old and has worked, before it was fashionable, as a day laborer, farmhand, dishwasher, waiter, sparring partner, newspaper reporter, foreign correspondent, and, since 1926, has supported himself and his family as a writer. From 1919 to 1927 he sent stories to American magazines without being able to sell one until the *Atlantic Monthly* published a story called "Fifty Grand." During this time the *Little Review* published several things, but were unable to pay for them, and he was selling stories, articles, and poems to magazines published in France and in Germany. Since he was a young boy he has cared greatly for fishing and shooting. If he had not spent so much time at them, at ski-ing, at the bull ring, and in a boat, he might have written much more. On the other hand, he might have shot himself.

He would rather read than do anything else except write, and nothing can make him so happy as having written well. He has been very lucky in his life and would like his luck to hold a little while longer.

KEY WEST, FLORIDA

Location: Georges Schreiber, *Portraits and Self-Portraits*, Speiser and Easterling-Hallman Foundation Collection of Ernest Hemingway, Thomas Cooper Library, University of South Carolina.

Blurb on broadside for *Spain in Flames* (February 1937). (facing)

This pro-Loyalist documentary movie was shown at the Cameo theater in New York.

★★★★ EXTRA ✕✕✕✕✕✕ CAMEO ✕✕✕✕✕✕ EXTRA ★★★★

NEWS FLASHES

Vol. II. No. 3   FEBRUARY, 1937   New York, N. Y.

SPAIN IN FLAMES

Thousands Massacred by Fascists

with Hitler-Mussolini Help

SEE STIRRING MOVIE

Direct from Civil War Front

Women and children lying dead in the streets of Madrid are seen in the new film document at the Cameo, "SPAIN IN FLAMES."

After a fiery introduction, spoken by the Spanish Ambassador, Fernando de los Rios, the film shows:

THE ABDICATION OF ALFONSO.
THE RISE OF THE REPUBLIC.
SUPPRESSION OF THE ASTURIAN MINERS.
THE VICTORY OF THE "POPULAR FRONT."
THE INVASION BY FRANCO'S MOORISH TROOPS.
HITLER'S & MUSSOLINI'S PLANES OVER SPAIN.
THE SIEGE OF THE ALCAZAR.
THE RECRUITING OF THE LOYALIST ARMY.
THE DEFENSE OF THE GUADARRAMA SECTOR.
THE EVACUATION OF CHILDREN FROM MADRID.
THE INCENDIARY BOMBING AND BOMBARDMENT OF THE CITY.
THE FIRING AND SHATTERING OF HOMES.
"LA PASSIONARIA," WOMAN LEADER IN ACTION.
AMAZING SPECTACLE OF TRAGEDY & HEROISM.

PRESS ACCLAIMS SCOOP FILM

of Spain's Fight for Freedom

N. Y. HERALD TRIBUNE: "Terrifying . . . gripping . . . eloquent . . . powerful . . . enormously convincing. . . . Should be seen by everyone."

N. Y. TIMES: "Vivid picture of what has happened, and is happening overseas. Grim and horrible record of the ravages of the Civil War."

N. Y. WORLD-TELEGRAM: "Only an army without a shred of humaneness or in the final stages of desperation could resort to such unnecessary butchery."

N. Y. POST: "It is horrible and stirring. It expresses the spirit and optimism of the workers of a nation which won't be oppressed."

ERNEST HEMINGWAY (Author of "Farewell to Arms"): "No one, no matter what their political belief or religious faith, could see this picture without experiencing a profound feeling of pity, horror and indignation."

NOW PLAYING CAMEO

42ND STREET, EAST OF BROADWAY

25 CENTS TO 1 P. M.
—— WEEK DAYS ——
Midnight Show Saturdays

Location: Speiser and Easterling-Hallman Foundation Collection of Ernest Hemingway, Thomas Cooper Library, University of South Carolina.

"Fascism Is a Lie," *New Masses* 23 (22 June 1937): 4. Location: Speiser and Easterling-Hallman Foundation Collection of Ernest Hemingway, Thomas Cooper Library, University of South Carolina.

In this speech delivered to the American Writers' Congress, New York City, 4 June 1937, Hemingway adopts the stance of the veteran talking: "You" means "I." The address begins and ends with a disquisition on the responsibilities of writers in wartime.

A writer's problem does not change. He himself changes, but his problem remains the same. It is always how to write truly and, having found what is true, to project it in such a way that it becomes a part of the experience of the person who reads it.

There is nothing more difficult to do, and because of the difficulty, the rewards, whether they come early or late, are usually very great. If the rewards come early, the writer is often ruined by them. If they come too late, he is probably embittered. Sometimes they only come after he is dead, and then they cannot bother him. But because of the difficulty of making true, lasting writing, a really good writer is always sure of eventual recognition. Only romantics think that there are such things as unknown masters.

Really good writers are always rewarded under almost any existing system of government that they can tolerate. There is only one form of government that cannot produce good writers, and that system is fascism. For fascism is a lie told by bullies. A writer who will not lie cannot live or work under fascism.

Because fascism is a lie, it is condemned to literary sterility. And when it is past, it will have no history except the bloody history of murder that is well known and that a few of us have seen with our own eyes in the last few months.

A writer, when he knows what it is about and how it is done, grows accustomed to war. That is a serious truth which you discover. It is a shock to discover how truly used to it you become. When you are at the front each day and see trench warfare, open warfare, attacks, and counter-attacks, it all makes sense no matter what the cost in dead and wounded—when you know what the men are fighting for and that they are fighting intelligently. When men fight for the freedom of their country against a foreign invasion, and when these men are your friends—some new friends and some of long standing—and you know how they were attacked and how they fought, at first almost unarmed, you learn, watching them live and fight and die, that there are worse things than war. Cowardice is worse, treachery is worse, and simple selfishness is worse.

In Madrid, where it costs every British newspaper £57 or say $280 a week to insure a correspondent's life, and where the American correspondents work at an average wage of $65 a week uninsured, we of the working press watched murder done last month for nineteen days. It was done by German artillery, and it was highly efficient murder.

I said you grow accustomed to war. If you are interested enough in the science of it—and it is a great science—and in the problem of human conduct under danger, you can become so encompassed in it that it seems a nasty sort of egotism even to consider one's own fate. But no one becomes accustomed to murder. And murder on a large scale we saw every day for nineteen days during the last bombardments of Madrid.

The totalitarian fascist states believe in the totalitarian war. That, put simply, means that whenever they are beaten by armed forces they take their revenge on unarmed civilians. In this war, since the middle of November, they have been beaten at the Parque del Oeste, they have been beaten at the Pardo, they have been beaten at Carabanchel, they have been beaten on the Jarama, they have been beaten at Brihuega, and at Cordoba, and they are being fought to a standstill at Bilbao. Every time they are beaten in the field, they salvage that strange thing they call their honor by murdering civilians.

You have seen this murder in Joris Ivens's film, so I will not describe it. If I described it, it would only make you vomit. It might make you hate. But we do not want hate. We want a reasoned understanding of the criminality of fascism and how it should be opposed. We must realize that these murders are the gestures of a bully, the great bully of fascism. There is only one way to quell a bully, and that is to thrash him; and the bully of fascism is being beaten now in Spain as Napoleon was beaten in that same peninsula a hundred and thirty years ago. The fascist countries know it and are desperate. Italy knows her troops will not fight outside of Italy, nor, in spite of marvelous material, are they the equal as soldiers of the new Spanish regiments. There is no question of them ever equaling the fighters of the international brigades.

Germany has found that she cannot depend on Italy as an ally in any sort of offensive war. I have read that von Blomberg witnessed an impressive series of maneuvers yesterday with Marshal Badoglio, but it is one thing to maneuver on the Venetian plain with no enemy present, and another to be outmaneuvered and have three divisions destroyed on the plateau between Brihuega and Trijueja, by the Eleventh and Twelfth International Brigades and the fine Spanish troops of Lister, "Campesino," and Mera. It is one thing to bombard Almeria and take an undefended Málaga given up by treachery, and another to lose seven thousand troops before Cordoba and thirty thousand in unsuccessful assaults on Madrid. It is one thing to destroy Guernica and another to fail to take Bilbao.

I have talked too long. I started to speak of the difficulty of trying to write well and truly, and of the inevitable reward to those who achieve it. But in a time of war—and we are now in a time of war, whether we like it or not—the rewards are all suspended. It is very dangerous to write the truth in war, and the truth is also very dangerous to come by. I do not know just which American writers have gone out to seek it. I know many men of the Lincoln Battalion. But they are not writers. They are letter writers. Many British writers have gone. Many German writers have gone. Many French, and Dutch writers have gone; and when a man goes to seek the truth in war he may find death instead. But if twelve go and only two come back, the truth they bring will be the truth, and not the garbled hearsay that we pass as history. Whether the truth is worth some risk to come by, the writers must decide themselves. Certainly it is more comfortable to spend their time disputing learnedly on points of doctrine. And there will always be new schisms and new fallings-off and marvelous exotic doctrines and romantic lost leaders, for those who do not want to work at what they profess to believe in, but only to discuss and to maintain positions—skillfully chosen positions with no risk involved in holding them, positions to be held by the typewriter and consolidated with the fountain pen. But there is now, and there will be from now on for a long time, war for any writer to go to who wants to study it. It looks as though we are in for many years of undeclared wars. There are many ways that writers can go to them. Afterward there may be rewards. But that need not bother the writer's conscience. Because the rewards will not come for a long time. And he must not worry about them too much. Because if he is like Ralph Fox and some others he will not be there to receive them.

**Preface, *All Good Americans* by Jerome Bahr (New York: Scribners, 1937).
Location: Speiser and Easterling-Hallman Foundation Collection of Ernest Hemingway, Thomas Cooper Library, University of South Carolina.**

There is no information about Hemingway's connection with Bahr (1909–90). Hemingway may have written this preface as a favor to Scribners.

These stories by Jerome Bahr need no preface. Their solid, youthful worth, their irony, their humor, their peasant lustiness, and the Pieter Brueghel quality of the country and the people that Mr. Bahr has made, need no comment by another writer. Along with many other excellencies they will be apparent to any one who reads the book. Why, then, should the book have a preface? It should not have one.

But, when you are a young writer, the only way you can get a book of stories published now is to have some one with what is called, in the trade, a name write a preface to it. Otherwise you must write a novel first. A novel, even if it fails, is supposed to sell enough copies to pay for putting it out. If it succeeds, the publisher has a property, and when a writer becomes a property he will be humored considerably by those who own the property. He will be, that is, as long as he continues to make them money, and sometimes for a long time afterwards on the chance that he will produce another winner. But when he is starting out he is not humored at all and many natural, good story writers lose their true direction by having to write novels before they are ready to if they want to earn enough at their trade to eat; let alone to marry and have children. It is the same system by which young prizefighters are overmatched and destroyed because their managers need the money that the fight, which the fighter does not yet know enough to win, will bring.

So I am very glad to write a preface to Mr. Bahr's book if doing so will get it published. I think he is a fine honest writer with a talent which is both sturdy and delicate, and I apologize to the reader for the economic necessity of pointing out qualities that would be perceived without any pointing. Mr. Bahr, I am sure, will write a fine novel eventually—maybe he has it planned already—and I hope it will have great success and that he will live to become a gigantic publisher's property of the most enormous kind. In the meantime, he writes very good stories full of irony and empty of bitterness, writing them under the usual impossible circumstances of youth, and I feel very good that they are to be published and ask you to excuse the preface.

Introduction, *Atlantic Game Fishing* by S. Kip Farrington Jr. (New York: Kennedy, [1937]). Location: Speiser and Easterling Hallman Foundation Collection of Ernest Hemingway, Thomas Cooper Library, University of South Carolina.

Farrington (1905–83) was a stockbroker who became a leading sport fisherman and wrote books and articles on the subject. Hemingway's introduction is a model of his authoritative writing manner: he displays knowledge of technique, claims experience, and differentiates between the professionals and the fakers.

The development of big game angling was retarded for many years by inadequate tackle. It is, at present, in danger of being completely ruined as a sport through the development of too efficient tackle. This last phase has come on very fast.

The present very excellent tackle has been developed through the natural desire of the charter boat captains to have their clients catch big fish even though they were physically incapable of bringing them to gaff under the accepted rules of angling. So we now have unbreakable rods which can be rested on the gunwale of the boat whenever the angler's back gets tired while the boatman plays the fish with the boat; seventy-two thread lines, which, when wet can tow a good sized launch with the fish doing the towing; two handled reels with a one to one gear ratio which work like chain hoists and eliminates any necessity for pumping, and other interesting inventions.

Now an unbreakable rod is a marvellous thing but it is supposed to be held by the fisherman and not rested on anything if he is to consider that he caught the fish and not that it was caught by the boat and the boat captain. Seventy-two thread line automatically eliminates itself from sporting fishing because no man can lift, handle, hook the fish with, and support the weight during the fight, of a reel so big that it will hold enough seventy-two thread line to handle the first run of a five hundred pound tuna in the deep water off Bimini unless the reel is attached to the fishing chair in some such manner that the fish would be disqualified as being fairly caught. The low geared fishing reel which winches in the fish instead of merely taking up the line which the angler gains on the fish by pumping him up with the rod, has certainly come to stay as it enables people who are completely unable to raise a fish by pumping to practice this strenuous sport from which they would otherwise be barred. But if big game fishing is to remain in any manner a sport, that is, a contest of strength and endurance between man or woman and an oversize fish, these new fool-proofing improvements in tackle should not be abused.

Anglers have a way of romanticizing their battles with fish and of forgetting that the fish has a hook in his mouth, his gullet, or his belly and that his gameness is really the extreme of panic in which he runs, leaps, and pulls to get away until he dies. It would seem to be enough advantage to the angler that the fish has the hook in his mouth rather than the angler and that, if he is to be proud of catching him, he should pull him in by his own effort, holding the rod and reel in his hands and supporting the weight of it, if it is too heavy to hold, by a harness across his back or the small of his back, and that he should receive no aid from anyone until the leader, which cannot be reeled further because of its swivel, is brought to the hand of the boatman.

As long as anglers fish in that way all improvements in tackle are excellent. If a fisherman uses too heavy line he must automatically stand the punishment of the extra pull on his own back or shoulders. A heavy rod or too stiff rod will tire him proportionately on a huge fish. But if he rests the rod and reel on anything or in any way has them so tied that he does not support the pull of the fish but, rather, transfers it to the boat; he is not fishing—the boat is fishing for him. By the same standards, if anyone, the captain, or the mate, or any other angler touches the rod or reel to hook the fish or to help in any way during the course of the fight; the fish cannot be counted as caught by the angler. If records are to be made by fishermen who accept assistance during a fight with a fish; who deliberately rest their rods on the gunwales of the boat, rather than having it momentarily forced down, which could happen to anyone and in the days of the old style rods would have been penalized by the rod breaking; who tied their reels and rods to the fishing chair so that the chair bears the weight of the fish and his pull and the angler only cranks the reel; and who allow their fish to be shot for any reason or with any excuse; then big game fishing as a competitive sport becomes utterly ridiculous and should be taken seriously by no one.

The main trouble with big game fishing has always been that it was too expensive. Because of this it was practiced for many years by either the leisured class or men past the age of retirement from business. There were a few exceptions to this class of fishermen and when you look at the records of the biggest fish caught by fair methods you find they were almost all caught by the exceptions; those who took their fishing seriously, devoted much time to it, and brought to it a little something besides money and ambition. But it always seemed a shame to me that such a fish as the sailfish, one of the most beautiful in the sea, should be caught, say ninety times out of a hundred, by some fat-bellied old slob who did not even know the fish was good to eat or some rich young twirp who could not hit a ball out of the infield.

Then for a few recent years big game fishing was a young man's sport. It attracted athletes of all kinds and it was discovered that very large fish could be caught fairly and with no cheating in only a fraction of the time it was supposed to take to kill them with no lessening in the excitement of the fight. The difference was that the angler fought the fish at all times instead of spending the majority of his time resting. Now, with the new winches and unbreakable gear used unscrupulously, an angler who knows the effort and suffering involved in taking a large fish may see his record broken by someone who could not stay with a big fish ten minutes under regulation fighting conditions.

The sport is about due for a good house-cleaning if it is to continue as a sport. If it is to be merely a contest of egos on who can produce the largest fish at the dock by any means, then let it become ridiculous as soon as possible. A certain amount of people will always practice it as a sport of man or woman versus fish for their own pleasure, and their own satisfaction in winning by fair means. The sooner the others make themselves ridiculous the better. I knew an American sportsman in Havana who found the easiest way to beat the existing records was to buy his marlin from the market fishermen and then bring them in and hang them up at the Yacht Club. No one could compete with him. He caught them that way on twelve thread line in eight hundred fathoms of water and was, I believe, just about to go to nine thread line when someone obtained an affidavit from a market fisherman who had sold him a fine four hundred pound fish for twenty-three dollars, and he left town.

Perhaps if we can get enough fishermen of that type into big game fishing, we can get some of the overhead back by selling fish to them. That may be the next development in the sport.

Seriously, though, it is a grand sport. But it needs some simple and decent rules if it is to continue competitively. If it isn't to continue competitively, it will be all right with me. I would like to go back to fishing for fun and take a day off and go snapper fishing over by the concrete ship.

Blurb on back dust jacket, *Beat to Quarters* by C. S. Forester (New York: Little, Brown, 1937). Location: Special Collections, Georgetown University Library.

Hemingway's praise of Forester first appeared on the back jacket of this Horatio Hornblower novel; the statement was subsequently printed on the back cover of the paperback reprint of Forester's World War I novel, The General *(New York: Bantam, 1953).*

I recommend Forester to everyone literate I know.

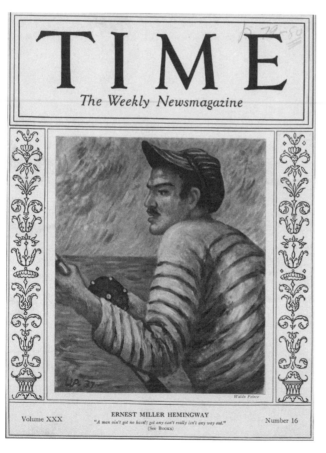

Hemingway's first appearance on the cover of *Time* (18 October 1937). Portrait by Waldo Peirce.

Blurb on front dust jacket of *The Chink in the Armour* by Mrs. Belloc Lowndes (New York: Longmans, Green, 1937).

Lowndes (1868–1947) was the author of The Lodger, *which Hemingway also admired. Woollcott (1887–1943) was a drama critic; Pearson (1880–1937) was an authority on the literature of crime.*

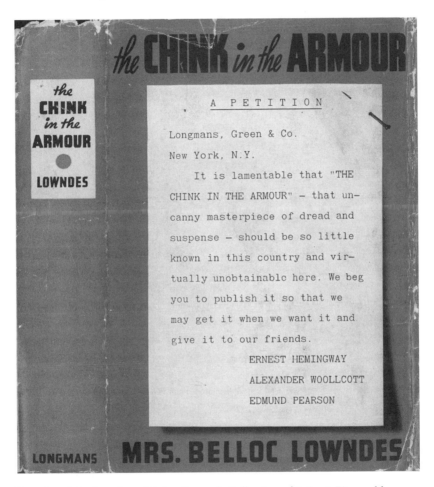

Location: Matthew J. and Arlyn Bruccoli Collection of F. Scott Fitzgerald, Thomas Cooper Library, University of South Carolina.

Endorsement for *Two Wars and More to Come* by Herbert L. Matthews (New York: Carrick & Evans, 1938), *New York Times Book Review,* 30 January 1938, 28.

Herbert L. Matthews (1900–1977) was a war correspondent with Hemingway in Spain. Matthews later stated, "Madrid, amidst many other happy memories, has that one for me, too—of great days with a man who exemplifies for me much that is brave and good and fine in a somewhat murky world. Ernest Hemingway is great-hearted and childish, and perhaps a little mad, and I wish there were more like him—but there could not be" (The Education of a Correspondent *[New York: Harcourt, Brace, 1946], 95). The ad omits the final sentence of Hemingway's cable: "I hope his office will keep some uncut copies of his dispatches in case he dies"(* Matthews, A World in Revolution *[New York: Scribners, 1971], 432–33).*

Reply to questionnaire, *transition* no. 27 (April–May 1938): 237. Location: Special Collections, Thomas Cooper Library, University of South Carolina.

Edited by Eugene Jolas, transition was a Paris-based little magazine of the surrealist persuasion. Hemingway's story "Hills Like White Elephants" had been published in the August 1927 issue of the periodical. Jolas submitted the following questions to the contributors: (1) What was your most recent characteristic dream (or daydream, waking-sleeping hallucination, phantasma)? (2) Have you observed any ancestral myths or symbols in your collective unconscious? (3) Have you ever felt the need for a new language to express the experiences of your night mind?

Answering your first question—I usually dream about whatever am doing at the time or what I have read in the paper; i.e., run into grizzly with wrong caliber shells for rifle; trigger spring sometimes broken, etc. when shooting; sometimes shoot very large animal of some kind I've never seen; or very detailed fighting around Madrid, house to house fighting, etc., after the paper; or even find myself in bed with Mrs. S... (not too good). Have had lovely experiences with Miss Dietrich, Miss Garbo and others in dreams too, they always being awfully nice (in dreams).

2. Second question, don't know much about.

3. I haven't ever felt this as would like to be able to handle day and night with same tools and believe can be done but respect anyone approaching any problem of writing with sincerity and wish them luck.

"Milton Wolff," *An Exhibition of Sculpture by Jo Davidson* (New York: Arden Gallery, 1938), 22. Hemingway's contribution was reprinted in *Jo Davidson Spanish Portraits* (New York: Printed by the Georgian Press, [1939]). Location for both: Speiser and Easterling-Hallman Foundation Collection of Ernest Hemingway, Thomas Cooper Library, University of South Carolina.

Davidson (1883–1952), who made portrait busts of many famous figures, referred to himself as a "plastic historian."

Nine men commanded the Lincoln and Lincoln-Washington Battalions. There is no space to tell about them here but four are dead and four are wounded and this is the head of the ninth and last commander, Milton Wolff, 23 years old, tall as Lincoln, gaunt as Lincoln, and as brave and as good a soldier as any that commanded battalions at Gettysburg. He is alive and unhit by the same hazard that leaves one tall palm tree standing where a hurricane has passed.

Milt Wolff arrived in Spain March 7, 1937, trained with the Washington Battalion and after reserve service at Jarama fought through the July heat and thirst of the blood bath that was called Brunete as a machine gunner. In September in the blowing dust of Aragon at the taking of Quinto and the storming of Belchite he was leading a section. In the Fifteenth Brigade's Passchendaele at Fuentes de Ebro he commanded a machine gun company. In the defence of Teruel fighting in the cold and the snow he was captain and adjutant. When Dave Reiss was killed at Belchite he took over the battalion and through the March retreat led it wisely and heroically. When finally it was surrounded and cut to pieces outside Gandesa he swam the Ebro with its remnants.

When what was left of the Fifteenth Brigade held at Mora del Ebro Wolff trained and reorganized his battalion and led it in the great offensive across the Ebro that changed the course of the war and saved Valencia. In the high mountains of Sierra Pandols, attacked repeatedly under the heaviest artillery and aviation bombardments of the war, they held their gains and turned them over intact to the Spaniards when the Internationals were withdrawn. He is a retired major now at twenty-three and still alive and pretty soon he will be coming home as other men his age and rank came home after the peace at Appomattox courthouse long ago. Except the peace was made at Munich now and no good men will be at home for long.

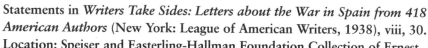

Statements in *Writers Take Sides: Letters about the War in Spain from 418 American Authors* (New York: League of American Writers, 1938), viii, 30. Location: Speiser and Easterling-Hallman Foundation Collection of Ernest Hemingway, Thomas Cooper Library, University of South Carolina.

The League of American Writers was formed in 1935 by the pro-communist American Writers Congress. Hemingway became a vice president—probably an honorary position—of the league in 1939. The writers who appeared in Writers Take Sides *were asked "Are you for, or are you against Franco and fascism?" and "Are you for, or are you against the legal government and the people of Republican Spain?" Of the 418 writers, 417 were anti-Franco and pro-Loyalist. Only historical novelist Gertrude Atherton (1857–1948) was pro-Franco.*

Telegram received from Paris, April 1:

RECENT HEAVY FIGHTING LOYALIST SPAIN MANY AMBULANCES CAPTURED OR DESTROYED BY BOMBS STOP MANY SPANIARDS AND THREE THOUSAND AMERICAN VOLUNTEERS FIGHTING FOR IDEALS DEAR ALL OF US SEVERELY HANDICAPPED WANT OF TRANSPORTATION CARRY WOUNDED FROM FRONT TO

HOSPITALS BEHIND LINES STOP IN HEROIC BACK-TO-WALL DEFENSE WHICH
SPANISH REPUBLIC NOW MAKING IN HOPE SAVING SITUATION AND CHECKING
FASCISTS ITS BRAVE TROOPS SHOULDNT BE SUBJECTED ANY SUFFERING WHICH
RELATIVELY SMALL SACRIFICE FROM US CAN AVOID STOP THIS CRITICAL HOUR
IN WORLD STRUGGLE FOR DECENCY AGAINST MEDIEVAL BARBARISM AS MANI-
FESTED AUSTRIA ELSEWHERE STOP IF YOU SEND CONTRIBUTION MEDICAL
BUREAU AND NORTH AMERICAN COMMITTEE TO AID SPANISH DEMOCRACY
381 FOURTH AVENUE NEW YORK THEY WILL CABLE MONEY THEIR PARIS REP-
RESENTATIVE WHO WILL GET AMBULANCES TO FRONT IN THREE DAYS STOP
GIVE QUICKLY STOP

signed

ERNEST HEMINGWAY

VINCENT SHEEAN

LOUIS FISCHER

# # #

ERNEST HEMINGWAY (*Farewell to Arms, To Have and Have Not*): Just like any
honest man I am against Franco and fascism in Spain.

Introduction, *Quintanilla* (New York: Museum of Modern Art, 1938).
Location: Museum of Modern Art. Reprinted, with three other Hemingway
pieces, in Quintanilla's *All the Brave* (New York: Modern Age, 1939), 7–11.
Location: Speiser and Easterling-Hallman Foundation Collection of Ernest
Hemingway, Thomas Cooper Library, University of South Carolina.

*The second of Hemingway's discussions of Quintanilla's politics and art was
published when the Loyalist cause was in peril.* All the Brave *includes three
additional Hemingway pieces, reprinted here, which are more about his own
war experience than about Quintanilla's work.*

A year ago today we were together and I asked Luis how his studio was
and if the pictures were safe.

"Oh, it's all gone, he said, without bitterness, explaining that a bomb had
gutted the building.

"And the big frescoes in University City and the Casa del Pueblo?"

"Finished," he said, "all smashed."

"What about the frescoes for the monument to Pablo Iglesias?"

"Destroyed," he said. "No, Ernesto, let's not talk about it. When a man
loses all his life's work, everything that he has done in all his working life, it
is much better not to talk about it."

These paintings that were destroyed by the bomb, and these frescoes that were smashed by artillery fire and chipped away by machine gun bullets were great Spanish works of art. Luis Quintanilla, who painted them, was not only a great artist but a great man. When the Republic that he loved and believed in was attacked by the fascists, he led the attack on the Montana Barracks that saved Madrid for the government. Later, studying military books at night while he commanded troops in the daytime, he fought in the pines and the grey rocks of the Guadarrama; on the yellow plain of the Tagus; in the streets of Toledo, and back to the suburbs of Madrid where men with rifles, hand grenades, and bundled sticks of dynamite faced tanks, artillery, and planes, and died so that their country might be free.

Because great painters are scarcer than good soldiers, the Spanish government ordered Quintanilla out of the army after the fascists were stopped outside Madrid. He worked on various diplomatic missions, and then returned to the front to make these drawings. The drawings are of war. They are to be looked at; not written about in a catalogue.

There is much to say about Quintanilla, and no space to say it, but the drawings say all they need to say themselves.

From *All the Brave*

I wrote this [the preface for the Museum of Modern Art Catalogue] and left for Spain on the eighteenth of last March. Mr. Elliot Paul,[1] who has known Quintanilla's work for many years and is much better qualified to write of it than I would ever be, had agreed to write a long critical introduction. I had promised to write a short one of a thousand words or less.

On the boat going over I tried to write this but it was quite impossible. I found that I had said what I felt about Luis Quintanilla in three hundred and fourteen words and in the face of what was happening just then in Spain the other thousand would not come. I did not worry particularly about the matter because I knew that, even if I should never be able to furnish a further introduction, there was this short one, and there would be a fine long one by Elliot Paul. Then, too, the things to see were Luis's drawings.

For a while in the months of March and April the Spanish war went very badly. I was always sure of an ultimate victory by the government; but there were many days when it looked as though long before that victory should be achieved a great many of us would be released from any necessity to write prefaces.

It was on one of those days, one of the very worst of those days, that I received a cable from New York saying that unless the publisher received the introduction by a certain date he would cancel the contract. So that night I wrote the introduction which follows and sent it off.

April 18, 1938, Somewhere in Spain
They are marvelous drawings. Quintanilla is a great Spanish artist and an old friend. He fought in the revolution and he fought in the war. I should now sit at the typewriter and write about how great he is as an artist, man, soldier, and revolutionary. But the typewriter is not going very well this evening.

Elliot Paul will write you all about the great painter Quintanilla is and I will bear testimony that his work has all been destroyed. I have seen the wreck a bomb made of his studio and looked at what artillery and machine gun fire did to his frescoes in University City. They are gone, all right, along with a lot of other things; along with too many other things. And what is there to be done about all this? Nothing. You can shut up and forget it. Which Quintanilla has done. Also he has gone on working.

Now if there were three candles to write this by instead of two candles it would probably be a brighter and more cheery introduction. You need good light to write introductions by. That is how they differ from dispatches. You can write dispatches by any sort of light but introductions need a better light and more time. So if anybody does not like this introduction, let them write an introduction of their own and I will be glad to sign it for them.

At this point in the introduction there should be a little literature about what it means to a man to have all his life's work destroyed. So at this point we will omit that bit of literature and take it for granted that nobody thinks it is funny for all the work a man has done in his life to be destroyed. Is that all right?

We will just take it for granted that it is unfortunate.

Now what comes next in an introduction? Certainly; that is it. The comparison with Goya. So let us just skip that too. Enough people will make that without our having to put it into this introduction and the candles are getting low.

So what comes now in an introduction to drawings of war? There certainly should be some reference to war itself. What do you think of war, Mr. Hemingway? Answer: I find it unpleasant. I have never liked it. But I have a small talent for it.

Do you like drawings of war? Answer: no. But these are very good ones. You probably will like them.

What do you like in war? Answer: to win it and get it over with and have peace.

What would you do in that event? Answer: I would go to The Stork Club.

You are evidently not a serious fellow. Answer: perhaps not.

You should not speak with such levity on such serious subjects. Answer: just where are you talking from, yourself?

That was New York speaking, but this is Barcelona, and yesterday was Tortosa, and tomorrow will be Tortosa again, and it is very difficult to write an introduction when the only thing you can think about is holding the line of the Ebro. Compared to the necessity of holding the line of the Ebro everything, including drawings of war by a great artist and one of your best friends, seems like chicken crut, and that is what makes this an unpleasant and churlish piece of writing.

If it was not for that you could remember the old days when we worked hard in Madrid together. That summer—when I wrote a book and Quintanilla did his great etchings and we all worked hard in the day and met in the evening to drink beer in the Cervecería in the Pasaje Alvarez and Quintanilla explained quietly and simply to me the necessity for the revolution—is a long way away now. It seems so far away that it is like a different world. It is like the old world there was once when, seeing a signboard saying 350 kilometers to such and such a town, you knew that if you followed that road you would get to that town. While now you know that if you follow that road you will get killed.

All that makes a little difference in you, and tonight the writing is not easy.

But the publishers demand an introduction, or they will cancel a contract. That is all right. They will get their introduction. It is coming out on the paper all the time. A letter at a time. A word at a time, a page at a time it comes out as well as any toothpaste squeezes and probably reads as attractively as some of the viler toothpastes taste. All that is necessary is for the candles to hold out so you can see the keys. But here she comes, publishers, here comes the good old introduction and if you want five thousand words there are different forms of the same word that could be written five thousand times and still quite a lot of contempt be unexpressed.

So now let's see. How many words are there to be? Put in a few more words for the publisher. The reader does not need them because the reader can look at the pictures. They are nice pictures, too. Are they not, reader? That is something of what war looks like; a very small part of it. And you must not be shocked at the dead Moors or think that they are disgusting because there is one thing that you learn in war and that is that a dead enemy always smells good.

So now we are getting to the end of the candles and the end of the introduction, I hope you like the introduction, I hope you like the pictures; I hope the publisher has not been annoyed, it was just kidding you know, publisher old boy, old boy. I hope you like Mr. Quintanilla; if you meet him, give him my regards.

You see there are quite a lot of Americans strung out along the Ebro too, along with Belgians, Germans, Frenchmen, Poles, Czechs, Croats, Bulgarians, Slovenes, Canadians, British, Finns, Danes, Swedes, Norwegians, Cubans, and the best Spaniards in the world. They are all waiting there for the decisive battle of the war to commence. So now if the introduction stops, please don't mind.

It could easily go on much longer if I had learned the touch system so that I could write in the dark. But it would all be very much the same. Because everything except the Ebro seems very unimportant tonight.

ERNEST Hemingway

May, 1938, Somewhere in Spain

At best an introduction is only a literary curiosity so we will let that particularly churlish piece of writing stand. It is a good example of the peculiar, unattractive, surly righteousness which certain phases of war can produce in people. It is peculiarly unjust because I was angry at Luis when I wrote it. I was angry at him, I suppose, because he was alive and too many other people you were fond of died that month.

Luis Quintanilla is one of the bravest men that I have ever known. War is not his trade and there is no reason for him ever to do any more of it. He did enough of it. But this was the time when the Italians had been beaten again up the Ebro above Cherta. They had been beaten by Lister's division, and another division, the Third, of the old Fifth Army Corps, in a bitter ten-day battle; and we knew that they would never take Tortosa. We also knew that there was something rotten on the left flank and it went, very suddenly, with old Duran holding all the mountain in between, and after ten days you had to give them what they never could have taken. At such times people become very bitter and unjust. Afterwards you apologize. So I apologize to Luis, and to Luis only. He knows the sort of thing we are talking about and he understands.

Then there is the reference to The Stork Club. That looks like levity and levity is unpardonable in a serious writer. I have learned that, because when I have committed levity it has never been pardoned. A serious writer should be quite solemn. If you joke about things, people do not take you seriously. These same people do not know there are many things you could not go through and keep sane if you do not joke, so it will be well to explain that levity has not been committed. The reference to The Stork Club is serious.

When you have sat at a table and been served a plate of water soup, a single fried egg and one orange after you have been working fourteen hours, you have no desire to be anywhere but where you were, nor to be doing anything but your work, but you would think, "Boy, I'll bet you could get quite a meal at The Stork tonight."

And when you would lie in the dark sometimes, with no company but the pictures in your head of what you had seen that day and all the other days, it was all right and there was always plenty to think about—military, political and personal. But sometimes you would think about how nice and noisy it would be at The Stork now, and that if you were at The Stork you would not have to think at all. You would just watch the people and listen to the noise.

In the old days in Madrid when Quintanilla and Elliot Paul and Jay Allen and I lived there, there were many places where you could eat as well as you could do at The Stork and have just as pleasant a time. But food is scarce in Madrid now and there are very few good things to drink. Hunger is a marvelous sauce and danger of death is quite a strong wine, they say, but under hunger the stomach shrinks so that when you finally get a chance at a series of decent meals you have much appetite in the eyes but no capacity for eating; and you become so used to danger that there is no exhilaration in it, only annoyance.

You keep The Stork, though, as a symbol of how well you would like to eat. Because this war in Spain is not being fought so that everyone will be reduced to a level of blockade rations but so that everyone can eat as well as the best.

There should be a lot about the old days in this, but a strange thing about the war is that it destroys the old days. Each day wipes out each other day and by the time you have two or three hundred days of it in the same scene where once you lived in peace, the memories, finally, are as smashed as the buildings. The old days and the old people are gone and nostalgia is something that you read about in books.

Later on, perhaps, it all rebuilds just as the buildings are rebuilt. It was all very simple in the old days. The old days were so simple that now they seem almost pitiful. If you want to have it simple now, you can do one thing: take orders and obey them blindly. That is the only simplicity that is left now.

If you are a writer and, now that you have seen it, you want to get some of it down before it should cauterize itself away, you must renounce the luxury of that simplicity. In writing you have to make your own mistakes. So now you are all ready to make them for awhile.

I would like to hope that, in writing from now on about this war, I will be able to do it as cleanly and as truly as Luis Quintanilla draws and etches. War is a hateful thing. It is inexcusable except in self-defense. In writing of it, a writer should be absolutely truthful because, of all things, it has had the least truth written of it.

There are various reasons for this. One is that it is very dangerous to see much of it, and anyone seeing very much of it at first hand will be either wounded or killed. If those at it are not wounded or killed, they are apt to become brutalized so that they lose their sensitivity to normal reactions. Or they can become so frightened that their reactions are not normal either. To write about it truly you have to know a great deal about cowardice and heroism. For there is very much of both, and of simple human endurance, and it is a long time since anyone has balanced them truly.

I envy Quintanilla very much that he has his drawings made. For now I have to try to write my stories.

Ernest Hemingway

1. American expatriate writer in Paris and coeditor of *transition*.

The frontispiece for *All the Brave* is Quintanilla's self-portrait with Jay Allen, Elliot Paul, and Hemingway.

Blurb on back dust jacket for *The Lincoln Battalion* by Edwin Rolfe (New York: Random House, 1939).

Rolfe (1909–54), a journalist for the Daily Worker *and a poet, was a member of the Abraham Lincoln Battalion. In his 1939 book he recalled: "Among the American visitors, the outstanding one, and the one best loved by the Lincoln boys was, with [Herbert L.] Matthews, Ernest Hemingway. The presence of this huge, bull-shouldered man with the questioning eyes and the full-hearted interest in everything that Spain was fighting for instilled in the tired Americans some of his own strength and quiet unostentatious courage. They knew he was himself a veteran of one war, that he still carried in his own body the steel fragments of an old wound; and the fact that such a man, with so pre-eminent a position in the world, was devoting all of his time and effort to the Loyalist cause did much to inspirit those other Americans who were holding the first-line trenches" (70).*

Location: Collection of Matthew J. and Arlyn Bruccoli.

Blurb on front dust jacket of *In Place of Splendor: The Autobiography of a Spanish Woman* by Constancia de la Mora (New York: Harcourt, Brace, 1939).

De la Mora (1906–50)—who was married to Gen. Ignacio Hidalgo de Cisneros (1894–1966), the leader of the Republican air force—served as head of the Foreign Press Office.

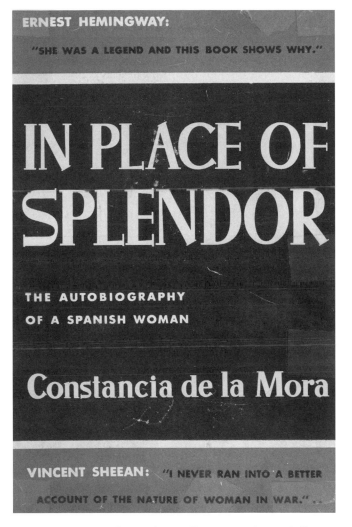

Location: Speiser and Easterling-Hallman Foundation Collection of Ernest Hemingway, Thomas Cooper Library, University of South Carolina.

Foreword, *Men in the Ranks* by Joseph North (New York: Friends of the Abraham Lincoln Brigade, 1939).

Joseph North (1904–76) covered the Spanish Civil War for the Daily Worker, *the newspaper of the American Communist Party.*

All those who went from here to Spain to fight are home now. That is they are all home except the men who are stranded in Ellis Island, or in Franco's prison corrals, or those who made their permanent homes in Spain in plots of ground six feet long, a foot to three feet deep, with a fine view of the grass roots growing.

You can do something about the men stranded in Ellis Island by contributing to their defense which is being conducted by the American Committee for Protection of Foreign Born, 100 Fifth Avenue, New York City. The Friends of the Lincoln Brigade will look after the prisoners still held by the fascists with the money that you contribute, and eventually they will be exchanged. You can do nothing for the dead except honor them in the way they would choose to be honored: by seeing that no man who fought in Spain should lack proper medical care and the opportunity to earn his living.

This pamphlet that Joe North has written will help that cause. It is not supposed to be a history of the Fifteenth International Brigade, and any collection of accounts of men who fought well is bound to be unfair to all others who fought well and are not mentioned. But I am sure that any man who fought in the Fifteenth Brigade would rather be unmentioned in a book and have the profit of that book go to help his wounded comrades than to be praised for all posterity in a book which had no useful purpose.

There will be books that will have a different use later. They will tell how the Brigades were recruited and organized, show the errors, explain why they were made and how they were corrected, and tell the true story of the building of the Lincoln and the Lincoln-Washington Battalions into the magnificent fighting units that, after the long period of holding on the Jamara heights, took Villanueva de la Canada in that hot July of 1937 and fought as well as any Americans ever fought in any battles, all through Brunete, the Aragon offensive, Teruel, Seguros de los Banyos and the Ebro.

The action of the Lincoln and Lincoln-Washington Battalions in Spain is already a part of American history. It is a fine part, and all who had a share in it can be proud within themselves as long as they live. As for those who died in Spain, the man whose name was given to the original battalion said all there is to say about them:

"The world will little note, nor long remember, what we say here, but it can never forget what they did here."

ERNEST HEMINGWAY
Visiting 15th International Brigade, December, 1937

FOREWORD

by ERNEST HEMINGWAY

All those who went from here to Spain to fight are home now. That is they are all home except the men who are stranded in Ellis Island, or in Franco's prison corrals, or those who made their permanent homes in Spain in plots of ground six feet long, a foot to three feet deep, with a fine view of the grass roots growing.

You can do something about the men stranded in Ellis Island by contributing to their defense which is being conducted by the American Committee for Protection of Foreign Born, 100 Fifth Avenue, New York City. The Friends of the Lincoln Brigade will look after the prisoners still held by the fascists with the money that you contribute, and eventually they will be exchanged. You can do

3

Location: Speiser and Easterling-Hallman Foundation Collection of Ernest Hemingway, Thomas Cooper Library, University of South Carolina.

Public Letter, American Committee for Protection of Foreign Born, circa 1939.

In a 1 February 1939 letter, Abner Green, publicity chair of the American Committee for Protection of Foreign Born, told Hemingway that his letter would be distributed as widely as possible. However, only one copy of this mimeographed public letter has been located (Collection of Waring Jones).

American Committee for Protection of Foreign ...

100 Fifth Avenue, New York City ★ Tel. — ALgonquin 4-2334

Dear Friend:

Patrick O'Donnell Read was born in Ireland forty-two years ago. During the World War he served in the Canadian Army and after he was honorably discharged he came to the United States. Last year he went from this country to Spain to volunteer his services in the International Brigades.

There were hundreds like Read, men of all walks of American life, of different political and economic opinions, who offered their lives to fight Fascism in Spain. These men are heroes. I saw them fighting in Spain, bringing honor to the name of America as an exponent of freedom and democracy. Instead of a hero's welcome on their return, however, Read and sixteen other veterans were stopped at Ellis Island and ordered excluded from this country because they are not citizens and failed to take the necessary steps to insure their reentry before leaving.

These seventeen veterans — their heroism and their value to American society — are being disregarded and cast into disrepute by an avalanche of legal technicalities that block their efforts to rejoin their families and friends. At the same time, a cruel fate awaits each and every one of them should they be returned to Europe to face eventual deportation to totalitarian countries.

We must do everything we possibly can to save these men. The American Committee for Protection of Foreign Born, which is defending them, informs me that legal steps can be taken in their behalf. The Committee informs me also that the defense of these men is seriously handicapped by the lack of necessary funds.

Approximately two hundred and fifty dollars is needed to enable one veteran to escape imprisonment and possible death in Germany or Italy or Greece or Yugoslavia. I feel sure that you, too, will want to do your utmost to help save these men. I am asking you to send your contribution to the American Committee for Protection of Foreign Born, 100 Fifth Avenue, New York City, immediately. It is the least we can do to help these heroes.

Sincerely yours,

ERNEST HEMINGWAY

uopwa - no. 16

Appeal for Aid to Loyalist Refugees [circa 1939], *Days of Anger, Days of Hope: A Memoir of the League of American Writers, 1937–1942,* by Franklin Folsom (Boulder: University Press of Colorado, 1994), 160. Location: Thomas Cooper Library, University of South Carolina.

This is the FBI file copy.

"*Unless s[om]e[th]ing [is] done soon; th[ere will be]*
deaths by the hundreds when winter comes."

So writes an anti-Nazi author about his colleagues who are facing their second winter in a French concentration camp. These are the men whose books you have read with pleasure, the men who brought the culture of Germany, Italy, Spain, Austria, Poland and Czechoslovakia into your home. These are the men whose fearless stand against fascism has brought them to suffering, persecution and exile.

Now their shelter is a concentration camp, their reward for resistance to Nazism, internment. Now they face another winter of cold, hunger, sickness. And the wonder is that every letter they write proves that spirit is still alive, their hatred of Hitler is still strong.

How much longer can such courage endure? Each letter tells how much the mere knowledge of the interest of American writers has served to maintain the morale of these refugees. But each letter also tells of their desperate need for help, their imminent danger of being seized by the Gestapo. Can we afford to let the voices they raised against oppression be silenced? As the picture on the reverse shows, "S.O.S.!" is the cry that comes to us from across the Atlantic.

This cry no longer comes from some 20 writers, thanks to $13,200 which was raised at a dinner we held on October 17th, in cooperation with a committee of leading publishers. Passage to Mexico has been bought for these fortunate exiles. But at least 75 others are awaiting our help. It now costs $600 per person to get them safely out of France to Mexico; while they wait in Lisbon for their chance to board the over-crowded boats, they must live. They must have food, money, medicine. And they count on us, democratic Americans, to bring them to the safety of the New World.

Can you fail to hear their cry this Christmas? "S.O.S!" They will be grateful for whatever contribution you can make towards the best gift we can send them—security, safety and a chance to write again.

THE NATIONAL BOARD OF THE LEAGUE OF AMERICAN WRITERS, INC.
(*Officers of the National Board are:* Donald Ogden Stewart,
PRESIDENT; Ernest Hemingway, Langston Hughes, Dorothy
Parker, Meridel LeSueur, George Seldes, Vincent Sheean, John
Steinbeck, and Richard Wright, VICE-PRESIDENTS.)

"On the American Dead in Spain," *New Masses* 30 (14 February 1939):
3. Reprinted in *Somebody Had to Do Something: A Memorial to James
Phillips Lardner* (Los Angeles: James Lardner Memorial Fund, 1939). Location for both: Speiser and Easterling-Hallman Foundation Collection of
Ernest Hemingway, Thomas Cooper Library, University of South Carolina.

*Lardner, a son of Ring W. Lardner, was a reporter in Spain when he joined the
Loyalists; he was killed in September 1938.*

New Masses

VOLUME XXX   FEBRUARY 14, 1939   NUMBER 8

On the American Dead in Spain

THE DEAD sleep cold in Spain tonight. Snow blows through the olive groves, sifting against the tree roots. Snow drifts over the mounds with the small head-boards. (When there was time for headboards.) The olive trees are thin in the cold wind because their lower branches were once cut to cover tanks, and the dead sleep cold in the small hills above the Jarama River. It was cold that February when they died there and since then the dead have not noticed the changes of the seasons.

It is two years now since the Lincoln Battalion held for four and a half months along the heights of the Jarama, and the first American dead have been a part of the earth of Spain for a long time now.

The dead sleep cold in Spain tonight and they will sleep cold all this winter as the earth sleeps with them. But in the spring the rain will come to make the earth kind again. The wind will blow soft over the hills from the south. The black trees will come to life with small green leaves, and there will be blossoms on the apple trees along the Jarama River. This spring the dead will feel the earth beginning to live again.

For our dead are a part of the earth of Spain now and the earth of Spain can never die. Each winter it will seem to die and each spring it will come alive again. Our dead will live with it forever.

Just as the earth can never die, neither will those who have ever been free return to slavery. The peasants who work the earth where our dead lie know what these dead died for. There was time during the war for them to learn these things, and there is forever for them to remember them in.

Our dead live in the hearts and the minds of the Spanish peasants, of the Spanish workers, of all the good simple honest people who believed in and fought for the Spanish republic. And as long as all our dead live in the Spanish earth, and they will live as long as the earth lives, no system of tyranny ever will prevail in Spain.

The fascists may spread over the land, blasting their way with weight of metal brought from other countries. They may advance aided by traitors and by cowards. They may destroy cities and villages and try to hold the people in slavery. But you cannot hold any people in slavery.

The Spanish people will rise again as they have always risen before against tyranny.

The dead do not need to rise. They are a part of the earth now and the earth can never be conquered. For the earth endureth forever. It will outlive all systems of tyranny.

Those who have entered it honorably, and no men ever entered earth more honorably than those who died in Spain, already have achieved immortality.

ERNEST HEMINGWAY.

"The Writer as a Writer," *Direction* 2 (May–June 1939): 3. Location: Harry Ransom Humanities Research Center, University of Texas, Austin.

This issue of Direction *served as the program for the Third American Writers' Congress, New York City, 2–4 June 1939.*

It was in a room on the fifth floor of the Majestic Hotel in Barcelona last April and Jim Lardner, pale, good looking, immensely serious about himself and the world and the world and himself, but always quick smiling if you made a joke about either one, was going over and over the same question, "Where and how do you think I would really be most useful here in the Spanish War?"

He had not yet made up his mind to join the International Brigade and part of the time he wanted you to argue him out of that intention and part of the time he hoped to be argued into it. It was very interesting to him and you can see how it would be. It was he who was doing the joining or the not joining. I did not think he should go into the Brigade at that time, although I believed he had a perfect right to if he wanted to.

"You really want to know where you would be most useful? Really useful? Not just to have someone argue with you?"

"Of course."

"Then go to Madrid and stay in it until it falls and after it falls stay on and then come out and write the truth about what happened. You have no registered political beliefs, you are not down as a sympathiser with the loyalist cause and you can stay there, see what happens and write the truth when all those who have either politics or are considered loyalist sympathisers will have to get out, be locked up, or shot."

"But you don't think Madrid will fall, do you?"

"No," I said. "But it always can fall. It can fall either through treachery or, if they make a big offensive with as much stuff as they used here in Catalonia, they can encircle it and starve it out. You would have to wait for that chance; go through the siege and be there to write about what happens when the Fascists come in. Otherwise no one will ever know. I think that is the most important thing any man in your position can do."

"It sounds very far fetched to me," Jim said. "I don't like to even talk about the possibility of them taking Madrid."

"Neither do I. But you asked me where I thought you could be most truly useful and I told you what I thought."

"How long would I have to be there?"

"Maybe a year. Maybe longer."

"And what if they never took Madrid?"

"Why you'd be o.k. If they never took Madrid the Government would have won the war. That's what you want, isn't it?"

"Yes. But I don't want to be a cheer leader. I want to take an active part."

"O.K.," I said. "You asked me where I thought you would be most useful. I told you. If you want to argue about joining the Brigade go on down and argue with Jimmy Sheean. I tell you in this war you do not have to write any propaganda for the side you believe in. All you have to do is write the truth and be there where you can write it. That is the most difficult thing to do. If no honest man is in Madrid to write about what really happens if it ever falls it will be one of the tragedies of history. You're ideal for the job and I think it's the absolutely most useful thing you could do. I'd do it but they would throw me in the can the minute they came in and all I could do would be write another book like Knoestler's.[1] That's as good a book as can be written on that subject. You could see it all."

"It sounds sort of like defeatist talk to me," said Jim. "And I think it is very far fetched."

Well, he joined the Brigade and soldiered well and everybody liked him and he was a fine kid and he ran into a fascist patrol, or onto a fascist post by mistake, in the night on the last night the Fifteenth Brigade was in the lines in the Sierra de Pandols and he was killed. His joining the Brigade was a fine example and he was a brave and cheerful soldier, if not a particularly skillful soldier, and he is dead.

There was no one in Madrid to do the job he could have done when the City fell to Franco and we have to depend for the truth on what happened there, and is happening there every day, on the dispatches of Mr. William Carney. As Jim said it seemed very far fetched at the time. But then writing is a very far fetched business and to be a writer you have to write even though you have to go far away or wait a long time to fetch the truth.

1. Apparently a misprint for Koestler. Arthur Koestler (1905–83) published *Spanish Testament*, an enlarged translation of his *Menschenopfer Unerhört*, in 1937.

"Eulogy to Gene Van Guilder," *Idaho Statesman*, 2 November 1939, 4.

Van Guilder (1905–39), who had been killed in a hunting accident, was a Sun Valley, Idaho, friend of Hemingway's. Lines from this eulogy appear on the monument to Hemingway in Sun Valley.

You all know Gene. Almost every one here is better equipped to speak about him and has more right to speak of him than I have. I have written down these thoughts about him because if you trusted yourself simply to speak about Gene there might be a time when you would be unable to go on.

You all know that he was a man of great talent. He had great talent for his work, for writing and for painting. But he had something much more than that. He had a great talent for living and for communicating his love and enjoyment of life to others.

If it was a fine bright day and you were out in the hills with Gene, he made it into a better day. If it was a dark gloomy day and you saw Gene, he made it a lot less gloomy. There weren't any bad days when Gene was around. He gave something of himself to all those who knew him or worked with him. And what he gave us all was very precious because it was compounded of the rarest elements. It was made up of true goodness, of kindliness, of fairness and generosity, of good humor, of tolerance and of the love of life. What he gave us he gave for good.

We have that from him always. When I heard that Gene had died I could not believe it. I cannot believe now. Yes, technically he is dead. As we all must be. But the thing he gave to those who knew him was not a thing that ever perishes and the spirit of Gene Van Guilder is not a thing that will perish, either.

Gene loved this country. He had a true feeling and understanding of it. He saw it with the eyes of a painter, the mind of a trained writer, and the heart of a boy who had been brought up in the west, and the better he saw it and understood it, the more he loved it.

He loved the hills in the spring when the snows go off and the first flowers come. He loved the warm sun of summer and the high mountain meadows, the trails through the timber and the sudden clear blue of the lakes. He loved the hills in the winter when the snow comes.

Best of all he loved the fall. He told me that the other night riding home in the car from pheasant hunting, the fall with the tawny and grey, the leaves yellow on the cottonwoods, leaves floating on the trout streams and above the hills the high blue windless skies. He loved to shoot, he loved to ride and he loved to fish.

Now those are all finished. But the hills remain. Gene has gotten through with that thing we all have to do. His dying in his youth was a great injustice. There are no words to describe how unjust is the death of a young man. But he has finished something that we all must do.

And now he has come home to the hills. He has come back now to rest well in the country that he loved through all the seasons. He will be here in the winter and in the spring and in the summer, and in the fall. In all the seasons there will ever be. He has come back to the hills that he loved and now he will be a part of them forever.

Endorsement for *Citizens* by Meyer Levin (New York: Viking Press, 1940), *The New York Times Book Review*, 31 March 1940, 13.

Levin (1905–81) wrote well-regarded social novels.

A fine and exciting American novel. . . . One of the best I have ever read.

Letter in "War Writers on Democracy," *Life* 8 (24 June 1940): 8.

Archibald MacLeish, poet, New Deal functionary, and Librarian of Congress, wrote an article for the 10 June 1940 issue of the New Republic *charging that the anti-war writers of the Twenties and Thirties—including Hemingway and himself—had weakened America's capacity to fight fascism. Hemingway and seven other writers (Maxwell Anderson, Robert E. Sherwood, Walter Millis, E. E. Cummings, C. Hartley-Grattan, Dalton Trumbo, and Richard Aldington) responded at the invitation of* Life.

Gentlemen:

Archibald MacLeish has blamed writers of his own generation for infusing the young generation with such cynicism and distrust that America today finds itself defenseless against Fascist aggression. Books by Hemingway, Dos Passos and others, he said, were completely honest and sincere in their hatred of war and the things that made war but they were "disastrous as education for a generation which would be obliged to face the threat of Fascism in its adult years." Such books, he declared, had immunized young Americans not only against phony patriotism but against all moral judgments of better or worse so that now all words and judgments are mistrusted and in their minds there is nothing real or permanent for which they are willing to fight. The moral and spiritual unpreparedness in arms he blamed squarely upon writers like himself and like you. Will you please rewire fifty or a hundred words of comment on Mr. MacLeish's statements?

THE EDITORS OF LIFE

Sirs:

MacLeish seems to have a very bad conscience. Having fought Fascism in every way that I know how in the places where you could really fight it, I have no remorse neither literary nor political. Suggest that MacLeish read my play *The Fifth Column* and see again the film *The Spanish Earth*. If MacLeish had been at Guadalajara, Jarama, Madrid, Teruel, first and second battles of the Ebro, he might feel better. Young men wrote of the first war to show truly the idiocies and murderous stupidity of the way it was conducted by the Allies and

Italy. Other young men wrote books that showed the same thing about the German conduct of the war. All agreed on war's vileness and undesirability. If the Germans have learned how to fight a war and the Allies have not learned, MacLeish can hardly put the blame on our books. Or do his highsounding words blame us because we never advocated a Fascism to end Fascism?

ernest hemingway

~

Preface, *The Great Crusade* by Gustav Regler, translated by Whittaker Chambers and Barrows Mussey (New York & Toronto: Longmans, Green, 1940). Location: Speiser and Easterling-Hallman Foundation Collection of Ernest Hemingway, Thomas Cooper Library, University of South Carolina.

Regler was a German Communist commissar in the International Brigade. Hemingway's preface to the novel boasts of his own participation in the Loyalist cause and his knowledge of the true gen: "General Lucasz, who is the General Paul of this book, asked me to make him a confidential report on what I saw when visiting this Hungarian general's front to make some film for a picture. I hope the report may have had something to do with his removal."

The Spanish civil war was really lost, of course, when the Fascists took Irun in the late summer of 1936. But in a war you can never admit, even to yourself, that it is lost. Because when you will admit it is lost you are beaten. The one who being beaten refuses to admit it and fights on the longest wins in all finish fights; unless of course he is killed, starved out, deprived of weapons or betrayed. All of these things happened to the Spanish people. They were killed in vast numbers, starved out, deprived of weapons and betrayed.

But this novel deals with the golden age of the International Brigades when all their gold was iron. It deals with the days when the Eleventh and Twelfth Brigades fought in defense of Madrid, at Boadilla del Monte, at the Arganda Bridge, in the Pardo, at Algora and Mirabueno, and finally at Guadalajara. No one has more right to write of these actions which saved Madrid than Gustav Regler. He fought in all of them.

You see the Eleventh Brigade was really the First Brigade. The Twelfth was the Second and so on. There were no first nine Brigades and there were never more than five. The Fifteenth Brigade, which in the time this novel deals with, contained the American Abraham Lincoln Battalion, was really the Fifth Brigade. It later became a very fine Brigade; one of the best in the army. But at the epoch this book deals with it had been almost destroyed in one single, idiotic, stupidly conceived and insanely executed attack in the hills above the Jarama River and, its morale low, it was holding a quiet stretch of front while a new Brigade was being built at the base.

The man who planned and ordered that attack was afterward shot when he returned to Russia. He should have been shot at the time. He was a Hungarian and he hated newspaper men. He had good reason to. For conditions on his front were so deplorable that as soon as they became known he was removed. General Lucasz, who is the General Paul of this book, asked me to make him a confidential report on what I saw when visiting this Hungarian general's front to make some film for a picture. I hope the report may have had something to do with his removal.

But while the Fifteenth Brigade spent their long, moral calvary of ninety-some days without being relieved in the now quiet hills above the Jarama, the Eleventh and Twelfth were fighting constantly. I was privileged to be with them a good part of this time.

They were two great Brigades. The Eleventh was German. They had nearly all had military training or fought in the war. They were all anti-Nazis. Most of them were Communists and they marched like the Reichswehr. They also sang songs that would break your heart and the last of them died on the Muela of Teruel which was a position that they sold as dearly as any position was ever sold in any war. But they were a little serious to spend much time with. Unless, of course, you were with Hans the Commander. Hans is a book to himself. We have too much together for me ever to risk losing any of it by trying to write about it. There is something about him in this book.

The Twelfth Brigade was where my heart was. There was Regler, who is the Commissar of this book. There was Lucasz, the General. There was Werner Heilbronn, who is the Doctor in this book. There were all the others. I will not name them. Some were Communists, but there were men of all political beliefs. They are all in this novel of Regler's and most of them are dead now. But until they died there was not one of them (that's a lie, there were a few) who could not make a joke in the imminent presence of death and who could not spit afterward to show the joke was real. We introduced the spitting test because it is a fact, which I discovered in early youth, that you cannot spit if you are really frightened. In Spain I very often could not spit after quite a good joke.

The jokes were never bravado. The jokes were because really brave men are almost always very gay and I think I can truly say for all those I knew as well as one man can know another, that the period of fighting when we thought that the Republic could win the Spanish civil war was the happiest period of our lives. We were truly happy then for when people died it seemed as though their death was justified and unimportant. For they died for something that they believed in and that was going to happen. Lucasz and Werner died as they die in this book. I never think of them as dead. I think I cried when I heard Lucasz was dead. I don't remember. I know I cried once when somebody died.

It must have been Lucasz because Lucasz was the first great loss. Everyone else who had been killed was replaceable. Werner was the most irreplaceable of all; but he was killed just afterward. And about crying let me tell you something that you may not know. There is no man alive today who has not cried at a war if he was at it long enough. Sometimes it is after a battle, sometimes it is when someone that you love is killed, sometimes it is from a great injustice to another, sometimes it is at the disbanding of a corps or a unit that has endured and accomplished together and now will never be together again. But all men at war cry sometimes, from Napoleon, the greatest butcher, down.

Gustav should have been killed when Lucasz was. It would have saved him much trouble, including the writing of this book. He would not have had to see the things that we have seen; nor the ones that we will have to see. He would not have had to be cured of a hole in the small of his back which uncovered the kidneys and exposed the spinal cord and that was so big, where the pound and a half piece of steel drove through Gustav's body from side to side, that the doctor pushed his whole gloved hand through in cleaning it.

He would not have lived to be put in a French concentration camp after he had fought France's battle in Spain and helped delay Germany's war on France, by the greatest holding attack in history. The Soviet Union was not bound by any pact with Hitler when the International Brigades fought in Spain. It was only after they lost any faith in the democracies that the Alliance was born.

If Gustav had been killed he would have been spared much suffering and much trouble. But he does not mind suffering, nor trouble, nor poverty, for himself. To Gustav those are only bad things to happen to others. He has, intelligently and unselfishly, the same bravery and immunity to personal suffering that a fighting cock has, which, wounded repeatedly, fights until it dies.

So Gustav will be all right as long as he is alive. The French have released him from concentration camp and admitted it was a mistake to have put him there. But Regler deserves to have a place to live and work: to be able to write and live with his wife and eat three meals a day. The best citizens we had came in the German migration of 1848, after another revolution failed. America is a big enough country to receive the Reglers who fought in Germany and in Spain; who are against all Nazis and their allies; who would honor America as much by living in it as we would aid them by granting them the right of asylum we have always accorded to those who have fought in their own land against tyranny and been defeated.

I have not written much about this book. It is to be read; not written about. Alvah Bessie wrote a book, a true, honest, fine book about the Fifteenth Brigade in the last phase the Brigade went through. In spite of the heroism and the wonderful fight they made in the Ebro diversion, it is no more typical or true account of the complete role of the International Brigades than an account of the retreat from Moscow would give you a true picture of Austerlitz or Wagram. We never had any Austerlitz. But we did have Madrid, Arganda, and Guadalajara. A great part of the men who made the good Brigades (there were bad ones too) immortal as some of the finest fighting units in history, were dead before Mr. Bessie joined what was left of the Fifteenth Brigade on their retreat from Aragon. The Brigades had the same numbers after Teruel, but the men were different.

The Ebro diversion was a great thing and Bessie writes truly and finely of all that he could see of it and he saw enough for one man. But Guadalajara, Arganda and Madrid were victories, and it is a good thing, to give those people who are opposed to Fascism hope, that these victories should be told now as Regler tells them: truly.

The greatest novels are all made-up. Everything in them is created by the writer. He must create from knowledge, of course, unless his book is to be a tour de force. There have been great tours de force too: *The Red Badge of Courage* and *Wuthering Heights*. But the authors of such books are usually poets who happen to be writing prose. But there are events which are so great that if a writer has participated in them his obligation is to try to write them truly rather than assume the presumption of altering them with invention. It is events of this importance that have produced Regler's book.

Camaguey, Cuba: 1940

Introduction, *Henrietta Hoopes* (New York: Knoedler Galleries, 1940).

Hoopes (1904–96) interested Hemingway because of her bullfight art, but his introduction is not serious: "basket is what my youngest boy said papa called the car when it would not start on a cold morning."

She paints bullfight pieces, horse pieces with the riders in pink coats, portraits and objects. People in Spain have liked the bullfight pieces and the funny ones are good jokes done from the outside. I'd rather she painted them straight and I like the bullfight etchings better. I like the portraits more and the objects the best. The eggs are very fine. The eggs would make a necessary part of a very fine bullfight picture. Maybe sometime she will go back and look at them again and put the eggs in various baskets. The baskets (basket is what my youngest boy said papa called the car when it would not start on a cold morning) wear heavy jackets that shine bright in the sun and when you get eggs in those baskets and in the bull too you can see a bullfight. This is getting very metaphysical so suppose you look at the pictures. They are very various and varied. Good luck to Henrietta Hoopes. It sounds like the start of a very gay poem. But I can't finish it. She will though.

Location: Speiser and Easterling-Hallman Foundation
Collection of Ernest Hemingway, Thomas Cooper Library,
University of South Carolina.

Invitation, Dinner Forum on "Europe Today," 9 October 1941.

Hemingway did not speak at this forum. The sponsors were the American Committee to Save Refugees, the Exiled Writers Committee of the League of American Writers, and the United American Spanish Aid Committee. Lillian Hellman (1906–84) was a playwright and Stalinist.

Lillian Hellman and Ernest Hemingway

and

The Committee of Sponsors

request the pleasure of your company

at a

DINNER - FORUM

on

"EUROPE TODAY"

Guest Speakers

DIANA FORBES-ROBERTSON

ERIC KNIGHT   JOHANNES STEEL
EMIL LENGYEL   PIERRE VAN PAASSEN
EDGAR SNOW   MAX WERNER

at the

HOTEL BILTMORE
Madison Avenue at Forty-Third Street

at seven o'clock
Thursday, October the Ninth
Nineteen hundred and forty-one

R. S. V. P.   Program on Page Two

Location: Speiser and Easterling-Hallman Foundation Collection of Ernest Hemingway, Thomas Cooper Library, University of South Carolina.

"Ernest Hemingway: Why He Selected 'The Short Happy Life of Francis Macomber,'" in *This Is My Best,* ed. Whit Burnett (New York: Dial Press, 1942), 22. Location: Matthew J. and Arlyn Bruccoli Collection of F. Scott Fitzgerald, Thomas Cooper Library, University of South Carolina.

Whit Burnett (1899–1973) was a founder and editor of Story *magazine. His anthology was widely read. Hemingway reluctantly cooperated.*

Referring to the many kinds of stories in his collection, *The Fifth Column and the First 49 Stories,* Ernest Hemingway listed "The Short Happy Life of Francis Macomber" first in the seven stories of his own he liked the best. . . . A laconic man, Mr. Hemingway wrote on May 12 to the editor of this anthology:

"If you want to print a selection of my work, I would suggest your reprinting 'The Short Happy Life of Francis Macomber' and simply say that Mr. Hemingway thought that this was as reprintable as any other of his stories."
Cuba   ERNEST HEMINGWAY
June, 1942

Golden Jubilee Greetings, *Program of the Cincinnati Symphony Orchestra*, 23–24 March 1945. Location: C. E. Frazer Clark Collection, University of Maryland Libraries.

Hemingway had no connection with either the Cincinnati Symphony Orchestra or the city of Cincinnati.

Felicitations to the Cincinnati Symphony Orchestra on its Golden Anniversary, and to its great conductor, Eugene Goossens, for their joint contribution to the art and culture of America.

Introduction, *Studio: Europe* by John Groth (New York: Vanguard, 1945). Location: Speiser and Easterling-Hallman Foundation Collection of Ernest Hemingway, Thomas Cooper Library, University of South Carolina.

Groth (1902–83) was a respected illustrator before and after World War II. He illustrated the 1946 World Publishing Company reprint of Hemingway's Men Without Women *(Location: Collection of Matthew J. and Arlyn Bruccoli), which includes "A Note on the Author by the Artist." One paragraph reads: "That morning, he showed me war. We jeeped past men and machinery moving up. Not comfortably, for jeep seats are not wide, and Hemingway is. (And there were canteens of cognac on each hip.) When we reached pill-boxes that had been captured the day before, he set up his canteens on the bank of a depression behind one of the boxes, making an impromptu bar. Infantry men stopped with him for a drink. They all knew him, but not as Ernest Hemingway the writer. They knew him as 'Pop.' He'd been with them in their drive across France. He'd been everywhere they had been. He didn't need any qualifications."*

John Groth used to sketch everybody and everybody was very pleased with it because he looked more like an artist than any good artist I had ever known looked. The men would look at the sketches and see just a lot of lines; but John looked so much like an artist they took it on trust. Everybody liked him and everybody thought he was crazy because he spent so much time in places where people who did not have to go were considered, fairly accurately, to have an odd mental structure if they went.

As well as sketching he wrote dispatches on a strange typewriter that he worked almost as slowly as a hand printing press using only the capital letters. I too believed him to be crazy and I liked him very much.

In a war you feel affection for anyone who does not look warlike. John looked so un-warlike that he inspired instant affection in anyone but the type of Public Relations Officer who, never having fired a shot, other than verbal,

John Groth provided this drawing of himself with Hemingway for the illustrated edition of *Men Without Women* (New York: World, 1946). Location: Collection of Matthew J. and Arlyn Bruccoli.

A Note on Ernest Hemingway

The first time I saw Ernest Hemingway was in early September, 1944. The First Army had edged into Germany. I reached the Fourth Division Headquarters in late afternoon. The Public Relations Officer told me that Hemingway was staying in a farmhouse in the Siegfried Line. He would take me there if I liked. I liked it very much—a chance to see Hemingway at war.

It was night; raining. There was shelling when we arrived at the farmhouse, which was only a darker shape in the surrounding blackness. A quickly opened and shut door, and we were in

11

in anger takes an almost sexual pleasure in feeling the weight of a Colt 45 pistol against his thigh and lives to the full his brief moment of command. There were fine PROs in the U.S. Army and there were despicable PROs and John's mere appearance could rouse the ones who sometimes seemed like imitations of men masquerading as officers to a fury that surely must have given them some of their most vivid moments in this last war in Europe.

Until I read the galley proofs of this book I did not know that John had not always worn that beard that so impressed us in the Schnee-Eifel. In the old days when I used to write articles for *Esquire* not favouring the build-up for this last war John used to make drawings for them. They were very different from his drawings in this book. I imagined him as a very rugged and uncompromising man with a pencil. The early drawings were as different from these as John as I imagined him and John when I finally saw him. The pre-war drawings always had someone pushing a bayonet through someone else and while that is doubtless very laudable in war it is hardly typical.

John's drawings are not designed to compete with anything. In spirit they seem to me to have some kinship with the illustrations for Grimm's Fairy Tales. Since the Schnee-Eifel was supposed to be where many of those fine stories happened there may be some sense in that. Reading his account of our home life in that same district it seems only slightly less fantastic than if Grimm had written it. I do not remember it that way. But nobody ever remembers it the way it was.

When you like someone as much as we liked John and respect his courage, good humour and sound humanity you should not be asked to write an introduction to his book and his drawings. He always reminded me of the good child who dies early in the book. I never saw him go off to the Third Battalion of the 22nd Infantry, who lived and died in the Schnee-Eifel under such conditions that a more or less visiting Major-General received a silver star for dropping in on them briefly on a day between the fighting when not a shot was fired, that I did not expect we would be burying him that night or the next day. But he always came back with the sketch book full of lines we could not understand.

These drawings may be as different from Bill Mauldin's great cartoons as Watteaus differ from Daumiers. But if John would have made them from any closer up front he would have had to have sat in the Krauts' laps.

What more should you say about him? He looked like someone who was understudying the man who would play Our Lord in a stream-lined Passion Play with North Germans instead of Bavarians. He was always brave, cheerful and discovering. He had a clean and credulous curiosity. Goodness and kindness shone from him and he had a child-like quality that reaches its full flowering in that unbelievable chapter about the girl who thought she had sinned, her mother thought she had sinned, even John finally seems to have thought maybe they had sinned, but I should not give away the plot.

I liked the part about the first days in France and about the break-through best. John only showed me a few of the pictures when he asked me to write the introduction. So this only holds for the ones I've seen. The others may be very different. I told him I was no good at introductions and he said, "But you can just say you saw me make some of these drawings."

I think that is said. But here it is again. I saw him make them on good days and bad days, when it was quiet and under really heavy artillery fire. None of us understood the sort of shorthand he sketched in. Most of us thought he was crazy. All of us liked him. All of us respected him. It was a very great pleasure to find what fine drawings they were when we finally got to see them.

August 25, 1945
San Francisco de Paula, Cuba

Foreword, *Treasury for the Free World*, edited by Ben Raeburn (New York: Arco, 1946). Location: Collecton of Matthew J. and Arlyn Bruccoli.

This foreword was written from the point of view of Hemingway the pundit and post-war statesman.

Now that the wars are over and the dead are dead and we have bought whatever it is we have it is a good time to publish books like this.

We have come out of the time when obedience, the acceptance of discipline, intelligent courage and resolution were most important into that more difficult time when it is a man's duty to understand his world rather than simply fight for it.

To understand we must study. We must study not simply what we wish to believe. That will always be skillfully presented for us. We must try to examine our world with the impartiality of a physician. This will be hard work and will involve reading much that is unpleasant to accept. But it is one of a man's first duties now.

It will be our duty, when we have sufficient valid knowledge, to disagree, to protest, even to revolt and to rebel and still work always toward finding a way for all men to live together on this earth.

It has been necessary to fight. It has been necessary to kill, to maim, to burn and to destroy. Certainly for a country whose continent has never been bombed we have done our share of bombing. We have possibly killed more civilians of other countries than all our enemies did in all the famous massacres we so deplore. There is really very little favorable difference to a man or a woman between being burned alive or stood against a wall and shot.

We have waged war in the most ferocious and ruthless way that it has ever been waged. We waged it against fierce and ruthless enemies that it was necessary to destroy. Now we have destroyed one of our enemies and forced the capitulation of the other. For the moment we are the strongest power in the world. It is very important that we do not become the most hated.

It would be easy for us, if we do not learn to understand the world and appreciate the rights, privileges and duties of all other countries and peoples, to represent in our power the same danger to the world that Fascism did.

We have invented the sling and the pebble that will kill all giants; including ourselves. It is simple idiocy to think that the Soviet Union will not possess and perfect the same weapon.

This is no time for any nation to have any trace of the mentality of the bully. It is no time for any nation to become hated. It is no time for any nation even to swagger. Certainly it is no time for any nation to jostle. It is no time for any nation to be anything but just.

In this new world all of the partners will have to relinquish. It will be as necessary to relinquish as it was necessary to fight. No nation who holds land or dominion over people where it has no just right to it can continue to do so if there is to be an enduring peace. The problems this brings up can not be examined in this foreword. But we must examine them and examine them intelligently, impartially and closing our eyes to nothing.

This book has one advantage. The various articles are not full of the knowledge after the fact of the use of the release of atomic energy. We need to study and understand certain basic problems of our world as they were before Hiroshima to be able to continue, intelligently, to discover how some of them have changed and how they can be settled justly now that a new weapon has become a property of a part of the world. We must study them more carefully than ever now and remember that no weapon has ever settled a moral problem. It can impose a solution but it cannot guarantee it to be a just one. You can wipe out your opponents. But if you do it unjustly you become eligible for being wiped out yourself.

In Germany our military courts have sentenced a sixty year old German woman to be hanged as one of a mob which brutally murdered American aviators who had parachuted to the ground in Germany. Why hang her? Why not burn her at the stake if we wish to make martyrs?

For the Germans know whether any sixty year old German women were ever killed by fighter pilots, on their way back from missions, coming down to strafe German villages. As far as I know we never hanged any pilots for going down on the deck and doing a little strafing. German civilians, strafed in Germany, feel much the same about it as Spanish civilians strafed in Spain by Germans or as American civilians would feel if the Germans had ever been able to strafe them.

Say you've been down on the deck; sometimes there were comic incidents. Often they looked comic from the air. Nothing blew up like ambulances (which proved the Germans carried munitions in them). Always plenty comic instances when you have command of the air. Comic to you. I believe in shooting up everything, myself, and getting it over with. (You shouldn't say that. That's too much like war.) But you cannot expect them not to be excited if you fall into their hands.

Air-Marshal Harris is on record as to what he wished to do to the German people. We were fighting the German people as well as the German army. The Germans fought the British people as well as the British army. The German army fought the Russian people and the Russian people fought back. That is war and to fight a war any other way is playing dolls.

But the secret of future peace is not in hanging sixty year old women because they killed fliers in hot blood. Hang or shoot those who starved and beat and tortured in cold blood. Hang or shoot those who planned the war and would plan another. Hang or shoot deliberate war criminals. Deal with the S.S. and the voluntary Party members as they should be dealt with. But do not make martyrs of sixty year old women who killed in anger against force which had become so strong it no longer had any conscience or any feeling of evil doing.

To win a war you have to do things that are inconceivable in peace and that are often hateful to those who do them. That is they are hateful for a while. Afterwards some people get used to them. Some get to like them. Everyone wants to do everything, no matter what, to get it over with. Once you are involved in a war you have to win it by any means.

The military, in order to maintain their status and certain safeguards of their status, would like to have war fought by rules. The air-forces steadily smashed through all these rules and developed a realistic war in which nations fought nations, not armies armies.

An aggressive war is the great crime against everything good in the world. A defensive war, which must necessarily turn to aggressive at the earliest moment, is the necessary great counter-crime. But never think that war, no matter how necessary, nor how justified, is not a crime. Ask the infantry and ask the dead.

We have fought this war and won it. Now let us not be sanctimonious; nor hypocritical; nor vengeful nor stupid. Let us make our enemies incapable of ever making war again, let us re-educate them, and let us learn to live in peace and justice with all countries and all peoples in this world. To do this we must educate and re-educate. But first we must educate ourselves.

San Francisco de Paula, Cuba
September 1945

Letter to Ernst Rowohlt, in *Rowohlts Rotblonder Roman* (Hamburg, 1947), 44. Location: Special Collections, Knox College Library.

This privately printed book celebrated the sixtieth birthday of Hemingway's German publisher.

December 18, 1946
My dear Ernst,

I was delighted to receive your letter which reached me in translation after some delay and was glad to know that you are well and back in business again. You certainly had a hell of a war and I am delighted that you were not one of the numerous Krauts that we killed in Schnee Eifel or Hurtgen Forest. Do not think that this is the language of the oppressive victor as you certainly killed many more of our boys at both of these places than we killed of you. (Glad we never killed each other.)

Please write to Anne Marie Horschitz[1] for me and tell her I look forward to having her translate my works again. She was the finest translator I ever had in any language.

Please keep in touch with me through my lawyer, Maurice J. Speiser, 630 Fifth Avenue, New York 20, N.Y., and let me know what conditions are and when you think it will be feasible to publish in Germany again. Then we can discuss making a deal. In the meantime I will not make any other deals with German publishers without getting in touch with you first.

However, please try to dig up a little money so that I will not have to be at the Kaiserhof[2] again waiting while you chase money all over Berlin.

    With warmest affection,

    Your old counter-comrade,

    ERNEST HEMINGWAY

    1. Having translated *In Our Time, The Sun Also Rises, Men Without Women,* and *A Farewell to Arms,* Horschitz continued as primary German translator of Hemingway's later works.

    2. Berlin hotel.

"Hemingway in the Afternoon," *Time* 50 (4 August 1947): 80.

This article included responses by Robert Penn Warren, William Faulkner, John P. Marquand, John Dos Passos, William Saroyan, and Katherine Anne Porter.

[*Time:* editorial note] Most of the authors who answered TIME's questions on the state of U.S. writing were interviewed by correspondents. Ernest Hemingway answered his questions by mail. He requested that both TIME's questions & his answers be published "since this has to do with my trade. You can say that when you saw me I was unshaven, needed a haircut, was barefoot, wearing a pyjama bottom and no top." The questions, and his replies:

What do you find wrong with present-day writing—or good about it? Why aren't we getting more significant writing?

    "Really good writing very scarce always. When comes in quantities everybody very very lucky."

Has postwar or atomic era had any influence on writers; has it had a tendency to dry them up creatively?

    "Writers dry up when their juice dries up. Atomic bomb probably as fatal to writers as cerebral hemorrhage or senility. Meantime good writers should keep on writing."

Which U.S. writers in your opinion are doing good work?

"Writers my generation mostly dead except Dos Passos going very good with *Number One*. Robert Penn Warren writing very well. First rate books by new writers that have read are *All Thy Conquest*, Alfred Hayes—*Never Come Morning*, Nelson Algren—*The Big Sky*, A. B. Guthrie Jr.—*The Assault*, Allen R. Matthews."

Which once-prominent ones have slipped or failed to measure up to early promise?

"Prefer not to answer this question. A writer has no more right to inform the public of the weaknesses and strengths of his fellow professionals than a doctor or a lawyer has.

Writers should stick together like wolves or gypsies and they are fools to attack each other to please the people who would exploit or destroy them. Naturally I know the weaknesses of my fellow professionals but that information is not for sale nor for free."

How much has the big money of slicks, Hollywood, radio, etc., taken writers away from serious personal themes?

"Most whores usually find their vocations."

Is a writer-Hollywood combination capable of doing good literary work?

"So far hasn't. But Hollywood has proven can make good pictures from good stories honestly written."

What is your own attitude toward writing for Hollywood.

"Never done it."

Do you detect any trends, or any new schools in recent U.S. writing? If so, what are they?

"Ask a professor."

Has the "Hemingway influence" declined? If so, what kind of writing are we heading for?

"Hemingway influence only a certain clarification of the language which is now in the public domain."

Endorsement for Parker "51," *Life* 24 (26 January 1948): inside front cover.

This manuscript passage is from Hemingway's foreword to Treasury of the Free World, *printed on pages 90–92.*

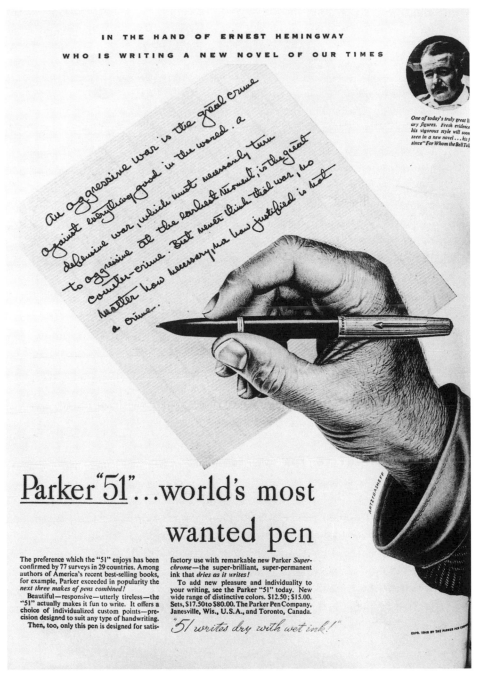

Location: Matthew J. and Arlyn Bruccoli Collection of F. Scott Fitzgerald, Thomas Cooper Library, University of South Carolina.

Introduction, *A Farewell to Arms* by Hemingway, illustrations by Daniel Rasmusson (New York: Scribners, 1948). Location: Speiser and Easterling-Hallman Foundation Collection of Ernest Hemingway, Thomas Cooper Library, University of South Carolina.

This is the only introduction that Hemingway wrote for a new edition of one of his books.

This book was written in Paris, France, Key West, Florida, Piggott, Arkansas, Kansas City, Missouri, Sheridan, Wyoming, and the first draft of it was finished near Big Horn in Wyoming. It was begun in the first winter months of 1928 and the first draft was finished in September of that year. It was rewritten in the fall and winter of 1928 in Key West and the final rewriting was finished in Paris in the spring of 1929.

During the time I was writing the first draft my second son Patrick was delivered in Kansas City by Caesarean section and while I was rewriting my father killed himself in Oak Park, Illinois. I was not quite thirty years old when I finished the book and the day it was published was the day the stock market crashed.[1] I always thought my father might have waited for this event, but, perhaps, he was hurried then, too. I do not like to make judgments since I loved my father very much.

I remember all of these things happening and all the places we lived in and the fine times and the bad times we had in that year. But much more vividly I remember living in the book and making up what happened in it every day. Making the country and the people and the things that happened I was happier than I had ever been. Each day I read the book through from the beginning to the point where I went on writing and each day I stopped when I was still going good and when I knew what would happen next.

The fact the book was a tragic one did not make me unhappy since I believed that life was a tragedy and knew it could only have one end. But finding you were able to make something up; to create truly enough so that it made you happy to read it; and to do this every day you worked was something that gave a greater pleasure than any I had ever known. Beside it nothing else mattered.

I had published a novel previously. But I knew nothing about writing a novel when I started it and so wrote too fast and each day to the point of complete exhaustion. So the first draft was very bad. I wrote it in six weeks and I had to rewrite it completely. But in the rewriting I learned much.

My publisher, Charles Scribner, who knows a great deal about horses, as much as a man probably should be allowed to know about the publishing business, and, surprisingly, something about books, asked me to write how I felt about illustrations and having a book illustrated. That can be answered quite simply: unless the artist is as good or better a painter or draftsman than the writer is a writer, there can be no more disappointing thing than for the writer to see the things and the places and the people that he remembers making drawn and put on paper by some one else who was not there.

If I could write a book that took place in the Bahamas I would like it to be illustrated by Winslow Homer, provided he did no illustrating but simply painted the Bahamas and what he saw there. If I were Guy de Maupassant, a good job to have dead or alive, I would like my work to be illustrated by the drawings and paintings of Toulouse Lautrec, some outdoor scenes of the middle time of Renoir and have them leave my Norman landscapes alone, because no painter ever did them better.

You could go on with other writers and what you would like to have if you were them. But all those writers are dead and all of those painters are dead too, along with Max Perkins and the other people that died last year. That is one good thing about this year; no matter who dies this year it can't be as bad as last year was or as 1944 or the early winter and spring of 1945. Those were vintage years for losing people.

When this year started in Sun Valley, Idaho, with champagne others paid for and people playing, seriously, some sort of game where they had to crawl under a stretched cord or a wooden stick without touching their over-inflated bellies, their noses, the straps on their Tyrolean jackets or other prominent features, I was sitting in a corner drinking our combined hosts' champagne with Miss Ingrid Bergman and I said to her, Daughter this is going to be the worst year that we have ever seen. (Have omitted the qualifying adjectives.)

Miss Bergman asked me why it was going to be such a bad year. She had enjoyed a number of good years herself and was loath to accept my view. I told her I would not explain in detail since I have only a limited command of the English language and my diction is faulty but that I knew it was a bad year from much uncorrelated, as yet, observation, and the sight of the wealthy and the gay crawling on their backs under this stretched cord or wooden stick did nothing to reassure. We let it go at that.

So this book was first published the day the market broke in 1929. The illustrated edition comes out this fall. Scott FitzGerald is dead, Tom Wolfe is dead, Jim Joyce is dead, (he the fine companion unlike the official Joyce of his biographers, who asked me one time, when drunk, if I did not think his work was too suburban); John Bishop is dead, Max Perkins is dead. Plenty of characters that should be dead are dead too; hung upside down outside of filling stations in Milano or hanged, well or badly in over-bombed German towns. There are all the non-name men dead too; most of whom liked life very much.

The title of the book is *A Farewell to Arms* and except for three years there has been war of some kind almost ever since it has been written. Some people used to say; why is the man so preoccupied and obsessed with war, and now, since 1933 perhaps it is clear why a writer should be interested in the constant, bullying, murderous, slovenly crime of war. Having been to too many of them, I am sure that I am prejudiced, and I hope that I am very prejudiced. But it is the considered belief of the writer of this book that wars are fought by the finest people that there are, or just say people, although, the closer you are to where they are fighting, the finer people you meet; but they are made, provoked and initiated by straight economic rivalries and by swine that stand to profit from them. I believe that all the people who stand to profit by a war and who help provoke it should be shot on the first day it starts by accredited representatives of the loyal citizens of their country who will fight it.

The author of this book would be very glad to take charge of this shooting, if legally delegated by those who will fight, and see that it would be performed as humanely and correctly as possible (some of the shoot-ees would undoubtedly behave more correctly than others) and see that all the bodies were given decent burial. We might even arrange to have them buried in cellophane or any one of the newer plastic materials. If, at the end of the day, there was any evidence that I had in any way provoked the new war or had not performed my delegated duties correctly, I would be willing, if not pleased, to be shot by the same firing squad and be buried either with or without cellophane or be left naked on a hill.

So here is the book after nearly twenty years and this is the introduction.

Finca Vigia, San Francisco de Paula, Cuba
June 30, 1948

1. *A Farewell to Arms* was published 27 September 1929, a month before the crash.

"Ernest Hemingway an Hans Kahle," *Heute und Morgen* **(1948): 497. Location: Deutsche Bibliothek, Frankfurt am Main. Location: C. E. Frazer Clark Collection, University of Maryland Libraries.**

Hans Kahle (1899–1947) was a German Communist who commanded a Loyalist division in the Spanish Civil War. After World War II he became the chief of police in Mecklenburg, East Germany. The editorial note and letter have been translated by Inge Kutt Lewis.

Hans Kahle, the first anniversary of whose death is on the 1st of September, was imprisoned in England in 1940. After a short stay on the Isle of Man, he was brought to Canada, where he stayed for nine months. During that time, he received the following letter from the American author Ernest Hemingway, with whom he fought in the Spanish Civil War and since then maintained a great friendship.

Heute und Morgen

Jahrgang 1948
Heft 8

HERAUSGEBER: WILLI BREDEL

Ernest Hemingway an Hans Kahle

Hans Kahle, dessen erster Todestag am 1. September ist, wurde 1940 in England interniert und nach einem kurzen Aufenthalt auf der Isle of Man nach Kanada gebracht, wo er neun Monate zubrachte. Während dieser Zeit erhielt er folgenden Brief von dem amerikanischen Schriftsteller Ernest Hemingway, mit dem er im spanischen Bürgerkrieg zusammen war und mit dem ihn seitdem eine große Freundschaft verband.

Lieber Hans!

Es tut mir schrecklich leid, zu hören, daß Du in einem Gefangenenlager bist. Wissen die Kanadier denn nicht, daß Du einer der wertvollsten lebenden Kämpfer gegen den Faschismus bist? Wissen sie denn nicht, daß Du ein Divisionsgeneral bist, der länger und erfolgreicher gegen den Faschismus gekämpft hat, als die ganze britische Armee während dieses Krieges? Ich jedenfalls weiß es, und ich werde alles tun, damit die höchsten Stellen es zu wissen bekommen.

Viel Wasser ist den Ebro entlang geflossen, seit wir ihn an jenem Tage kreuzten. Ich wollte, wir hätten solch einen Sport zweimal die Woche. Mit Whisky hinterher. Ich erinnere mich immer daran, wie wir hinterher glücklich wie die Kinder durch das Bombardement liefen, weil wir beide im selben Alter unsere Knabenzeit durchlebten in diesem großen Stadium der Unverwundbarkeit, der uns alten Soldaten eigen ist, statt des Stadiums der Gnade.

Hans, laß mich bitte wissen, was ich für Dich tun kann. Ich war kürzlich in New York, und da kam Duran und blieb drei Tage bei uns. Er korrigierte das Spanisch in meinem Buch, das im Oktober herauskommen wird. Die Buchgemeinschaft des Monatklubs hat es angenommen, und es wird eine erste Auflage von 200 000 Exemplaren haben. Das nennt man Glück. Ich werde Dir eine Kopie schicken. Es wird nicht so gut sein wie „Men against Metal", aber es sind Stellen darin, dir Dir gefallen werden. Es ist auch etwas über Dich darin.

Ich sende Dir einen Scheck und hoffe, daß Du ihn einlösen kannst. Solltest Du damit Schwierigkeiten haben, so schreibe mir bitte nach Sun Valley, Idaho, wo ich meine Kinder nächste Woche treffen werde. Schreibe mir, auf welche Weise ich Dir am besten Geld schicken kann. Ich weiß, daß Du nicht entmutigt bist, aber es ist doch immer ein blödes Gefühl, Gefangener zu sein. Ich wollte, Du würdest die 45. Division kommandieren, und ich hätte einen kleinen Posten in Deinem Stab.

Alles Gute, mein Lieber, schreib mir bitte nach Sun Valley und denk daran, daß ich immer Dein Freund und alter Kriegskamerad bleibe.

E. H.

497

Dear Hans,

I am very sorry to hear that you are in a prison camp. Don't those Canadians know that you are one of the most valuable living warriors against Fascism? Don't they know that you were a division general who has fought longer and more successfully against Fascism than the entire British army during this war? At least I know it, and I will do everything so that the highest level will know it, too.

Much water has flowed along the Ebro since we crossed it in those days. I wish we had such sport twice a week. Followed by whisky. I always remember how we ran, happy as children, though the bombardment, because we experienced our youth at the same age, in this great stage of invulnerability, which is peculiar to veterans, instead of the stage of grace.

Hans, please let me know what I can do for you. A short while ago I was in New York and Duran arrived and stayed three days with us. He corrected the Spanish in my book, which will be published in October. The monthly book club has accepted it and it will have a print run of 200,000 copies. That's what's called luck. I will send you a copy. It won't be as good as "Men against Metal," but there are some places which you will like. There is also something about you in it.

I'm sending you a check and hope that you can cash it. Should you have difficulties, please wrote to me at Sun Valley, Idaho, where I'll be meeting my children next week. Please write, too, what the best way is to send you money. I know that you are not discouraged, but it's still a silly feeling to be a prisoner. I wish you would command the 45th division and I had a small position on your staff.

All the best, my dear, write to me at Sun Valley, and remember that I am always your friend and old war comrade.

E.H.

Blurb for *The Price Is Right* by Jerome Weidman (New York: Harcourt, Brace, 1949), front flap of dust jacket. Location: Collection of Matthew J. and Arlyn Bruccoli.

The source for Hemingway's statement is unknown; it was subsequently printed on the front of the paperback (New York: Manor, 1973).

Weidman writes "just a little better than anybody that's around."

"The Position of Ernest Hemingway: Notes from a Novelist on His System of Work," *The New York Times Book Review,* 31 July 1949, 1.

Critic Maxwell Geismar (1909–79) had included a chapter, "Ernest Heming-way: You Could Always Come Back," in his Writers in Crisis: The American Novel Between Two Wars *(New York: Houghton Mifflin, 1942). His "Notes from a Critic on a Novelist's Work," the essay that accompanied Hemingway's response printed below, was collected in Geismar's* American Moderns: From Rebellion to Conformity *(New York: Hill & Wang, 1958).*

[*NYTBR* editorial note] Ernest Hemingway was in Italy when Mr. Geismar was asked to write the essay appearing on this page. In the hope of arranging a *transatlantic interview* between the Messrs. Hemingway and Geismar, a letter in questionnaire form was dispatched by *The Book Review* to Arnoldo Cortesi THE NEW YORK TIMES correspondent in Rome. Mr. Cortesi forwarded it to Mr. Hemingway. Mr. Hemingway pondered it and wrote his reply en route from Europe to his home in Cuba. The reply is published here in full.

I believe Mr. Cortesi explained to you why I was unable to answer your letter sooner.

Now, reading it over, I see it would take several thousand words of carefully considered writing to attempt an answer to all the things you bring up.

Let's give my personal life a miss. The only important things are that I should keep healthy and write as well as I can. This is my program for 1949 and as long after as possible.

A long time ago I found it was bad to discuss work you are engaged on. I know it does not work that way with all writers. But that is the way it works with me. It is not followed to be rude nor to be mysterious. It is a system of working.

Discussing other writers for publication is distasteful. Any good professional writer knows the strong points and the weaknesses of the other professionals. He is not under any obligation to point them out to the other writer's reading public. If the other writer is read his public must find the good in him. I see no reason to try to put him out of business by disillusioning anyone he may mystify.

Then, too, if a writer became a critic or entered other fields it could lead to grave humiliations. Imagine not being able to get your fast ball by Truman Capote or dropping a close decision to some Brooklyn Tolstoy. Think of how it could shake a writer's confidence to lose the Secretariat of Agriculture to Louis Bromfield in some little smoke-filled room or wake some morning to find that it was André Malraux who was managing De Gaulle instead of you or that Jean-Paul Sartre had won the hand of Simone De Beauvoir while you had been left at the post in the Fifth at Aqueduct. No, I think it is better just to write.

I once read an excellent book by Maxwell Geismar on American writing in which he knew so much about how and why I wrote that he had me groggy for what seemed like a decade (the smallest term used in Big Time Literature). How does Hemingway do it? I would mutter. This way? Or like Geismar says?

Finally I decided just to keep my left hand out and keep moving around and wait for Geismar to throw again. Maybe he can hit me with that same punch. Maybe he's got something new now. I want to make him throw though. Because if I keep on writing I can always hit him with a book.

I'm sorry I can't write that sort of piece with the writer's Views on things, and the Literary Scene, and which are my favorite books (the answer to that is the ones with the stiff covers), etc. because this ship is half way between Funchal, Madeira, and La Guayra, Venezuela, and there is a big wallowing, following sea and am writing this in the Chief Engineer's cabin and anyway I doubt if I could write it if I had an office of my own in the Chrysler Building and paid somebody to write it for me.

You're welcome to this though if it is any good to you and if you print any paragraphs from it please print them entire and as they are.

Yours very truly,

Ernest Hemingway

Introduction, *In Sicily* by Elio Vittorini, translated by Wilfrid David (New York: New Directions, 1949). Location: Speiser and Easterling-Hallman Foundation Collection of Ernest Hemingway, Thomas Cooper Library, University of South Carolina.

Conversazione in Sicilia (1942), regarded as the author's masterpiece, had been published in London in 1948 as Conversation in Sicily *with an introduction by Stephen Spender. Hemingway was not a personal friend of Vittorini.*

Elio Vittorini is one of the very best of the new Italian writers. He was born July 23, 1908, in Syracuse in Sicily and spent his boyhood in various parts of Sicily where his father was a station master on the railways of that island. He is not a regional writer, for Italy is certainly not a region, and Vittorini from the time he was old enough to leave home without permission at seventeen learned his Italy in the same way American boys who ran away from home learned their own country.

The Italy that he learned and the America that the American boys learned has little to do with the Academic Italy or America that periodically attacks all writing like a dust storm and is always, until everything shall be completely dry, dispersed by rain.

Rain to an academician is probably, after the first fall has cleared the air, H2O with, of course, traces of other things. To a good writer, needing something to bring the dry country alive so that it will not be a desert where only such cactus as New York literary reviews grow dry and sad, inexistent without the water of their benefactors, feeding on the dried manure of schism and the dusty taste of disputed dialectics, their only flowering a desiccated criticism as alive as stuffed birds, and their steady mulch the dehydrated cuds of fellow critics; such a writer finds rain to be made of knowledge, experience, wine, bread, oil, salt, vinegar, bed, early mornings, nights, days, the sea, men, women, dogs, beloved motor cars, bicycles, hills and valleys, the appearance and disappearance of trains on straight and curved tracks, love, honor and disobey, music, chamber music and chamber pots, negative and positive Wassrmanns, the arrival and non-arrival of expected munitions and/or reinforcements, replacements or your brother. All these are part of rain to a good writer along with your hated or beloved mother, may she rest in peace or in pieces, porcupine quills, cock grouse drumming on a bass-wood log, the smell of sweet-grass and fresh smoked leather and Sicily.

In this book the rain you get is Sicily. I care nothing about the political aspects of the book (they were many at the time) nor about Vittorini's politics (I have examined them carefully and to me they are honorable). But I care very much about his ability to bring rain with him when he comes if the earth is dry and that is what you need.

He has more books about the north of Italy that he knows and loves and about other parts of Italy. This is a good one to start with.

If there is any rhetoric or fancy writing that puts you off at the beginning or the end, just ram through it. Remember he wrote the book in 1937 under Fascism and he had to wrap it in a fancy package. It is necessarily wrapped in cellophane to pass the censor. But there is excellent food once you unwrap it.

Cortina D'Ampezzo, 1949

Endorsement for *The Man with the Golden Arm* by Nelson Algren (Garden City, N.Y.: Doubleday, 1949) in the *Book Find News* (January 1950), 5,

Nelson Algren (1909–81) and Hemingway had no personal connection; Hemingway admired Algren's novel about a drug addict, as well as his other books. Algren later wrote a nonfiction book titled Notes from a Sea Diary: Hemingway All the Way *(New York: Putnam, 1965).*

WIDE WORLD PHOTO

BY ERNEST HEMINGWAY AND CARL SANDBURG

EDITOR'S NOTE: Ernest Hemingway and Carl Sandburg need no introduction to readers of the *Book Find News*. Their candid comments on THE MAN WITH THE GOLDEN ARM are given here in full, without editorial excision. Mr. Hemingway, in fact, expressly stipulated that his statement be quoted "only in entirety and exactly as written."

"Into a world of letters where we have the fading Faulkner and where that overgrown Lil Abner Thomas Wolfe casts a shorter shadow each day, Nelson Algren comes like a corvette, or even a big destroyer when one of those things is what you need and need it badly and at once and for keeps. He has been around for a long time but only the pros knew about him.

"Now everybody will know about him because he will be available in sufficient quantity. Truman Capote fans grab your hats, if you have any, and go. This is a man writing and you should not read it if you cannot take a punch. I doubt if any of you can. Mr. Algren can hit with both hands and move around and he will kill you if you are not awfully careful. I hope this language is intelligible. We could always get some character in the Kierkegaard circuit to put it into acceptable literary terms. Mr. Algren, my boy, you are good."

        ERNEST HEMINGWAY

We could throw away Nelson Algren's three books, two novels and a collection of short stories, if they didn't have great qualities of insight into people, a heart of pity, a gift of cadence and song, and often when you near heartbreak he throws in comic relief. The interwoven police, politicians, gamblers and thieves, fixers and hustlers, the jargons of night clubs and prisons, these are here in THE MAN WITH THE GOLDEN ARM. Also the swarming and cramped lives underlying boy gangs, tenements, slums, "night without mercy," "children of the broken sky line." Algren makes his living grotesques so terribly human that their faces, voices, shames, follies and deaths, can linger in your mind with a strange midnight dignity. I join with Ernest Hemingway in hoping that Algren lives on, holds to his standards, and writes a long shelf of books.

        CARL SANDBURG

Location: New York Public Library.

Letter to Alberto Mondadori, 5 July 1950, in *Cinquantennio Editoriale di Arnoldo Mondadori, 1907–1957* (Verona, 1957), 228. Location: University of Miami, Coral Gables.

Alberto Mondadori (1914–76) was Hemingway's Italian publisher, in honor of whose firm—Arnoldo Mondadori—this fiftieth-anniversary volume was assembled. Hemingway wrote the letter in English: it was translated into Italian for the tribute volume and was retranslated for this collection by Fausto Pauluzzi.[1] The books that Hemingway recommends are by C. S. Forester (1899–1966), A. B. Guthrie Jr. (1901–91), and Jim Corbett (1875–1955).

5 luglio 1950/July 5, 1950

My dear Alberto,

Here are my presentations of the three books and the few words you requested. You do not owe me any compensation, I do this for affection. But I would like you to send the money to Father Francesco, the priest of Torcello,[2] telling him that it comes from me. He can use it as he best decides.

The African Queen
This is a strange, beautiful, disquieting book—which you can believe or not. Nonetheless it will take you into a land where you've never been before.
ERNEST HEMINGWAY

Big Sky
The times of mountain men in the Far West have never been narrated so well. And probably never will.
ERNEST HEMINGWAY

The man-eating leopard
It's the nicest book on hunting and being hunted that I ever read. It's so well written and so realistic that you get the impression you've lived it. It contains beauty, terror, realism.
ERNEST HEMINGWAY

Forgive my lateness. The drafts arrived with substantial delay. Then there was an accident at sea.

I hope you like the piece on Torcello. Please have Nanda[3] translate it and Adriano[4] illustrate it. Tell them that it was you who asked for such a short article; I wouldn't want anyone to think I had the impudence of compressing 1500 years into 150 words.

Many nice things to you and yours.
MISTER PAPA

1. Translator's note: "The letter is stylistically and grammatically perfect—consonant with what a well-educated Italian might produce. If Hemingway did not write Italian with facility, then one can assume that he either used an educated Italian intermediary to produce this version or that his manuscript letter was re-styled after its reception in Italy."

2. An island north of Venice.

3. Fernanda Pivano, who had also translated *Death in the Afternoon, A Farewell to Arms,* and other Hemingway books.

4. Typo for Adriana Ivancich, a young Italian woman with whom Hemingway was smitten. She did not illustrate any of his books, but her art was used on the dust jacket of *Across the River and Into the Trees.*

"'Hemingway Is Bitter about Nobody'—But His Colonel Is," *Time* **56 (11 September 1950): 110.**

Across the River and Into the Trees *was serialized in* Cosmopolitan *(February–June 1950) before book publication in September 1950. The disappointing critical reception of his novel—which nonetheless sold well—intensified Hemingway's contempt for reviewers and literary politics.*

[*Time* editorial note] Last year, in a rare revelation of his writing plans, Ernest Hemingway let it be known that he was writing a short novel: *Across the River and into the Trees.* . . . He was side-tracking work on a much longer novel to do so; the idea had come to him while recovering from serious illness. U.S. book circles were fascinated. As the story had it, Hemingway wanted to get some things down on paper that he had never managed to say before; *Across the River* was going to be the Hemingway credo in a nutshell. When a magazine version of the book appeared in *Cosmopolitan* earlier this year, it raised other questions. Wasn't the novel's hero a pretty thinly disguised version of Hemingway himself? What was Hemingway trying to say about Allied commanders in World War II? And—in view of the book's flaws—was Hemingway satisfied with it?

Time cabled some of these questions to Novelist Hemingway. His reply, cabled from Cuba:

Hemingway was ill with erysipelas, streptococcus, staphylococcus and anthrax infections in Cortina D'Ampezzo and in hospital in Padova. English spelling Padua. Received 13 million units of penicillin and 3,000,000 more later in Cortina.

His credo is to write as well as he can about things that he knows and feels deeply about.

The present novel is about love, death, happiness and sorrow. It is also about the city of Venice and the Veneto, which Hemingway has known and loved since he was a young boy.

The novel was written in Cortina d'Ampezzo; at Finca Vigia, San Francisco de Paula, Cuba; and in Paris and Venice.

It is the best novel that Hemingway can write, and he has tried to make a distillation in it of what he knows about the above subjects plus one other subject, which is war.

Hemingway is a writer not a soldier, nor has he ever claimed to be one. His son John, however, is a captain of infantry in Berlin and was severely wounded, a prisoner after he was wounded and later a hostage.

To resume answers. You have held me to $25 [cable tolls], so will omit details of any action or actions that Hemingway has participated in. His bad knee was acquired by an enemy *Minenwerfer* explosion which blew off the right knee cap.

Hemingway is bitter about nobody. But the colonel in his book is. Do you know any non-bitter fighting soldiers or any one who was in Hürtgen [Forest] to the end who can love the authors of that national catastrophe which killed off the flower of our fighting men in a stupid frontal attack?

Hemingway has no opinion in regard to General Eisenhower except that he is an extremely able administrator and an excellent politician. H. believes he did a marvelous job in organizing the invasion, if he was actually the man who organized it. H. means Hemingway, which I am tired of writing, and *he* in the above sentence means Eisenhower. Let us revere Eisenhower, Bedell Smith, the memory of Georgie Patton. But Hemingway refuses to revere Montgomery as man or soldier, and would rather be stood up against a wall and shot than make that reverence. He is the gentleman who took our gasoline to do what he could not do.

Hem admires General Omar Bradley and General Joseph Lawton Collins and loves the Army of the United States, but cannot love a chicken division when it is chicken. Love has its limits, but when it is given it is given for keeps though awful things may happen to it.

In regard to General Dwight D. Eisenhower, Hemingway, catching another question, only believes that all staff officers should have some combat experience to be familiar with their tools, which are, or were, members of the human race. In the last war, Hemingway, a word I'm getting sick of, was at sea on various projects for approximately two years under the orders of Colonel John Thomason, USMC, Colonel Hayne D. Boyden, USMC, Colonel John Hart, USMC. Then Hemingway left for the ETO and was accredited to the R.A.F. and specifically the tactical air force commanded by Air Marshal "Mary" Coningham. He flew with them a short time and then was accredited to the Third U.S. Army, from which he escaped while they were waiting around to go. They went very well once the infantry made the hole for them to go through, and held it open on both elbows.

Hemingstein was by this time with an infantry division which he loved [the 4th] and which had three fine regiments, wonderful artillery and good battalion of armor and excellent spare parts. Hemingstein was only a guest of this division, but he tried to make himself useful. He was with them through the Normandy break-through, Schnee Eifel, Hürtgen and the defense of Luxembourg.

About the other queries: there are 165,000 words done on the long book [on which Hemingway has been working since 1942]. Thirty thousand words done on poems.

About what he will concede [on the subject of *Across the River and into the Trees*]: we concede nothing, and what we take we hold.

For technicalities, the decorations that Hemingstein the writer holds, and the only ones that he respects, are the *Medaglia d'Argento al Valore Militare* and three *Croce al Merito di Guerra*.

Anything Mary [Mrs. Hemingway] told you over the phone I deny. Every word of this is accurate and true and I vouch for it and you can publish it in full or not at all.

"Important Authors of the Fall Speaking for Themselves," *New York Herald Tribune Book Review*, 8 October 1950, 4.

This statement is a notable example of Hemingway's skill at dramatizing himself as a writer by refusing to play the role of literary figure. It also proclaims the wide range of his interests. The Morning Telegraph *provided sporting news —mainly about horse racing. The two generals he corresponded with were Charles T. (Buck) Lanham and E. E. Dorman-Smith (Dorman-O'Gowan).*

My biographical data is in *Who's Who*. Am a resident of Finga Vigia—San Francisco de Paula—Cuba. About working: I work wherever I am and the earliest part of the morning is the best for me. I wake always at first light and get up and start working. There is a Springer Spaniel from Ketchum, Idaho named Black Dog who helps me to work. Three cats named Boise, Friendless's Brother, and Ecstasy give me valuable aid. A cat named Princessa, a smoke-grey Persian, helped me very much; but she died three weeks ago. I do not know what I will do if anything happens to Black Dog or to Boise; just go on working I suppose.

When I finish work I like to take a drink and go swimming. If I have worked well in the morning I try to get out fishing on the Gulf Stream in the afternoon.

In the old days I could read anything. But now I cannot read detective stories any more unless they are written by Raymond Chandler. Mostly I read biography, accounts of voyages that seem true, and military writing, good and bad. You learn about as much from one as from the other.

Fiction has been hard to read lately but I read it. Hope it will be a better year this fall.

Also read the *Morning Telegraph*, when it is obtainable, the *New York Times* and *Herald Tribune*.

Also read three French magazines that I subscribe to, some Italian weeklies, and a Mexican publication called *Cancha* devoted to Jai-Alai. Read the bull fight papers whenever some friend sends them. Read *Harpers*, *The Atlantic*, *Holiday*, *Field and Stream*, *Sports Afield*, *True*, *Time*, *Newsweek*, and the *Southern Jesuit*. Read *Sat. Eve. Post* whenever it has a serial by Ernest W. Haycox. Read a couple or more of Cuban newspapers a day and various South American literary magazines. Also read *Sport and Country* (British) and *The Field* (British), also any French books Sartre sends me. Read several books in Italian each year, some in manuscript and try to get the ones I believe in published.

Then there is correspondence. I write regularly to a general officer in the regular army and also to a former Lieut. Gen. in the British Army whom I knew when we were both young together in Italy. Also write regularly to about three friends. The rest of the correspondence is mostly casual or duty or business.

I don't play except for keeps.

Mary has masons, plasterers and painters in the house and I'm staying at sea until it's over. Also am supposed to be convalescing from a bad spill I had on the flying bridge, wet deck and very heavy sea, and my mate just swung her into the trough as I came over the rail. Got a five inch cut on the back of my head that went into the bone, a concussion, etc. Severed the artery and it took about five or six hours before we could get surgical treatment. Luckily Roberto Herrerra, an old friend, was running behind us. He has had five years of medicine and he and Mary contained the hemorrhage very well and his brother José Luis fixed it up.

All it amounts to is that I can't ski this year again. But can swim and walk and shoot and fish and work although José Luis told me not to.

But I am getting tired of getting hit on the head. There were 3 bad ones in '44–'45. Two in '43 and the others go back to '18. People think they come from carelessness. But they don't. At least none that I remember did.

Statement in "Success, It's Wonderful!" by Harvey Breit, *The New York Times Book Review*, 3 December 1950, 58.

Breit (1910–68) wrote a column of book and author news for The New York Times Book Review. *He and Hemingway were useful to each other.*

After I have written a book I only wish to see it published exactly as I wrote it and have as many people read it as possible. You write for yourself and for others. This last book was written for people, too, who had lived and would die and be capable of knowing the difference between those two states. It was also written for all people who had ever fought or would be capable of fighting or interested in it. It was written, as well, for people who had ever been in love or were capable of that happiness.

The fact that many people read the book of their own accord and that it is not a packaged product made me very happy. It has not, however, altered my way of life or any plans I may have. I hope to write as well as I can as long as I live. And I hope now to live quite a long time.

Many times critics do not understand a work when a writer tries for something he has not attempted before. But eventually they get abreast of it. The critic, out on a limb, is more fun to see than a mountain lion. The critic gets paid for it so it is much more just that he should be out on that limb than the poor cat who does it for nothing. Altogether I believe it has been quite healthy and the extremely dull thuds one hears as the critics fall from their limbs when the tree is shaken slightly may presage a more decent era in criticism—when books are read and criticized, rather than personalities attacked.

"Books I Have Liked," *New York Herald Tribune Book Review*, 3 December 1950, 6.

Hemingway and ten other writers—including Carl Carmer, Marchette Chute, Samuel Eliot Morrison, and Henry Comager—contributed to this survey.

ERNEST HEMINGWAY: *Collected Stories of William Faulkner; Mixed Company,* by Irwin Shaw; *Out of the Red,* by Red Smith.

"Hemingway Rates Charles for Gazette," *National Police Gazette* 66 (January 1951): 16. Location: Library of Congress.

Ezzard Charles had defeated over-age Joe Louis for the heavyweight championship on 27 September 1950.

San Francisco

Depaula, Cuba

H. H. Roswell

Publisher, Police Gazette (By Wireless)

Do not believe Charles is a great champion but admire the peak of condition he reached against a washed-up champion. Kid Tunero beat him badly in his home town spotting him twenty years and twenty pounds.

Do not believe he will be around for long unless we stop producing heavyweights. Admire his brave and skillful fight against Louis. But unfortunately remember back to Jeffries and Johnson and Sam Langford, Joe Jeannette and Sam McVey, and Charles does not rate to carry their used ....

Johnson was the best Negro heavyweight who ever lived. This is a dissenting opinion but Charles knows that it is true especially if he remembers the Tunero fight which he would like to forget.[1] He would not have lasted a round with Johnson, Tunney would have out-boxed and out-hit him and Dempsey or Firpo would have murdered him. Congratulate him on the Belt for me but tell him never to wear it if he is an honest man. I believe he is.

Yours very truly,

Ernest Hemingway

1. Evilia "Kid" Tunero, a Cuban, upset Charles in ten rounds on 13 May 1942.

Endorsement for Ballantine Ale in *Life* 31 (5 November 1951): 91. (overleaf)

Robert Benchley (1889–1945) was a heavy-drinking American humorist.

ERNEST HEMINGWAY, who has been called the greatest living American writer, is also internationally famous as a deep-sea fisherman. Since publication of *The Sun Al...* in 1926, his novels and short stories have enriched the literature of the English language consistently, year after year. His latest best seller is *Across the River and Into the...*

In every refreshing glass... Purity, Body and Flav

Location: Matthew J. and Arlyn Bruccoli Collection, Thomas Cooper Library, University of Sou

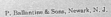

"Books I Have Liked," in "On the Books" by John K. Hutchens, *New York Herald Tribune Book Review,* 9 December 1951, 3.

Hemingway's list of books he had not obtained—because they were never written—displays his skill at the art of literary ridicule. The references to the two books by "FitzGerald" express his displeasure with the F. Scott Fitzgerald revival, evidenced by the Mizener biography and Budd Schulberg's novel The Disenchanted, *in which the central character is based on Fitzgerald. Combining them with a book by Melville—another writer whose critical reputation soared after his death—reinforces Hemingway's message that literary revivals are suspect.*

The other three apocryphal titles on Hemingway's list refer to Lillian Ross's hatchet-job profile of him in the New Yorker *("How Do You Like It Now, Gentlemen?" 26 [13 May 1950]: 36–62) and ridicule the intellectual reputations of Malraux and Sartre.*

Too late to appear with other "Books I Have Liked" lists in the Christmas Book Issue last week, the following letter from Cuba has arrived in the offices of this Review:

To the Editor:
    Here are three:
    The Consul at Sunset—Gerald Hanley
    The Broken Root—Arturo Barea
    Nobody Asked Me—Jimmy Cannon

This naming three is hard as you know. It was very hard to choose between Jimmy Cannon's book and Air Power in War by Lord Tedder. But since Lord Tedder's book had not been published in America, I chose Mr. Cannon's. Runner-up was The American Racing Manual—1951.
    Books I would have enjoyed reading but could not obtain here were:
    Longevity Pays: The Life of Arthur Mizener—by F. Scott FitzGerald
    The Shulberg Incident—by F. Scott FitzGerald
    The Critics: An Harpooner's Story—by Herman Melville
    Other fine books I was unable to get my hands on were:
    He and Lillian: The Story of a Profile—by Mary Hemingway
    Wisdom, Culture, God and I (3 vol.)—by André Malraux
    It Went Thataway: The Story of Existentialism—by Jean-Paul Sartre.
    I will stop now as there are so many good books one does not get to read these days.
    ernest hemingway

Preface, *A Hemingway Check List* by Lee Samuels (New York: Scribners, 1951). Location: Speiser and Easterling-Hallman Foundation Collection of Ernest Hemingway, Thomas Cooper Library, University of South Carolina.

Samuels lent Hemingway money and collected his books, but he wasn't much of a bibliographer. Hemingway's preface is about the theft or destruction of his literary property—not about his published work.

Lee Samuels is a man, who, with no wish to profit from it, finds and collects all that you have written and then lost or forgotten. He not only finds them. He gives you copies of them for better or for worse. Finally they are to be given to a library. It is such a disinterested action that it is impressive to the point of being almost incredible in these times.

It is too easy to remember sending a story to a limited edition publisher[1] (payment nil) and asking the return of the manuscript as it was the only copy you had. A few years later you were asked to authenticate the manuscript (which was accompanied by a letter requesting its return), in a Chicago bookstore where you had gone to buy something to read on the train.

That was the most disabusing transaction except for the constant theft of any first editions from the house by uninvited guests and by the guests of people to whom one had loaned the house. The first of the early first editions was small and fitted easily into a guest's pocket. There was another that was a little large. But not too large to slip under a guest's coat.

Then there was the problem of the disposal of what you have written by people one lives with.

The simplest way to dispose of anything in a periodical is to have the periodical thrown away in the interests of housekeeping. This reached its climax in a town called Key West, Florida. The disposal of manuscripts was ably accomplished by taking them out of your filing cabinets and putting them in cardboard boxes where they were eaten by mice, rats and roaches. This, with the aid of the climate, was almost infallible. It was as successful in destruction as the incinerator and it made no smoke nor ashes. Poems also disappeared without a trace. They are still missing.

There were always other ways of disposing of what the man a woman is married to writes including the loss of everything the husband had written and not yet published (original manuscript, typewritten copy and carbons; each in its separate folder) through having a suitcase stolen in the Gare de Lyons in 1922. A man's wife was bringing the manuscript and carbons for him to work on during a Christmas Vacation from working for The Toronto Star, INS and Universal Service at the Lausanne conference. The suitcase was stolen while she went out to buy herself a bottle of Vittel water.

But you do not marry a woman for her ability to care for manuscripts and I truly felt sorrier for how awfully she felt than I did for the loss of everything I had written. She was a lovely and loyal woman with bad luck with manuscripts. Anyway one story was not lost. It was called "My Old Man" and Lincoln Steffens had sent it out to a magazine from which it was duly returned. It thus became my literary capital. We used to call it "Das Kapital."

Of course Lee cannot find these things that were lost; and I have lost plenty myself: unassisted. But he has shown that he can find anything existent for whatever use it may have. I wish to thank him for his inexhaustible patience and for his kindness.

Finca Vigia
San Francisco de Paula
Cuba, 11/8/50

1. *Today Is Friday* (Englewood, N.J.: As Stable, 1926).

Preface, *Reginald Rowe* (New York: Wellons Gallery, 1952).

Hemingway's praise of Rowe (b. 1920) is cute: "When children, cats and dogs respect a painter you may be sure that he is doing something serious."

Reggie Rowe is our neighbor in Cuba. You could not ask for a nicer neighbor nor for a boy who paints better every year. It is pleasant to look out the door in the morning when you are working and see Reggie in an old straw hat and a pair of Navy shorts solving his problems of light and shade and the different grays and greens that we both love. I like to watch the puzzled expression he has when he paints because as long as an artist is puzzled he has a chance. The children of the village all watch him paint with great respect and many of them see their houses and the white dust of the road for the first time when he paints them. The cats and the dogs watch him with respect too. They do not understand what he is doing. But they can tell that it is important. When children, cats and dogs respect a painter you may be sure that he is doing something serious.

The light in Cuba is very strange. People do not realize that it is almost that of the upper Sudan and that in latitude Cuba is south of Karachi, India. The sun of Provence shines north of Boston and still it can blind you in the Midi. Reggie has worked with this problem of light, trying to solve it and show what it does at all hours. Each year he finds something that is new and true.

Finca Vigia
San Francisco de Paula, Havana
January, 1952

Reginald Rowe

FEBRUARY 18 TO MARCH 1, 1952

HOURS 10-6
FRIDAY to 8 P.M.

WELLONS GALLERY
70 EAST 56 STREET, NEW YORK

Location: Speiser and Easterling-Hallman Foundation Collection of Ernest Hemingway, Thomas Cooper Library, University of South Carolina.

"A Tribute to Mamma from Papa Hemingway," *Life* 33 (18 August 1952): 92–93.

By 1952 the Hemingway act had taken over the genius. This statement on Marlene Dietrich is a cringe-making combination of rhetoric and pretentious simplicity: "Since she knows about love, and knows that it is a thing which exists or does not exist, I value her opinion there more than that of the professors."

The following comments on Marlene were written specially for Life by Novelist Ernest Hemingway. Like all his other friends, she calls him "Papa." He calls her sometimes "Mamma" and sometimes "Kraut."

She is brave, beautiful, loyal, kind and generous. She is never boring and is as lovely looking in the morning in a GI shirt, pants and combat boots as she is at night or on the screen. She has an honesty and a comic and tragic sense of life that never let her be truly happy unless she loves. When she loves she can joke about it; but it is gallows humor.

If she had nothing more than her voice she could break your heart with it. But she has that beautiful body and the timeless loveliness of her face. It makes no difference how she breaks your heart if she is there to mend it.

Hemingway and Dietrich on shipboard; she is holding a copy
of his *The Fifth Column and the First Forty-nine Stories* (1938)
Location:. Hemingway Collection, John F. Kennedy Library.

She cannot be cruel nor unjust but she can be angry and fools bore her and she shows it unless the fool is in bad trouble. Anyone who is in serious enough trouble has her sympathy.

If this makes her sound too perfect, you should know that she can destroy any competing woman without even noticing her. She does it sometimes for fun and then tosses the man back where he belongs. She has a strange, for these times, code that will not let her take a man away from another woman if the woman wants him.

We know each other very well and are very fond of each other. When we meet we tell each other everything that has happened in between times and I don't think we ever lie to each other unless it is very necessary and on a temporary basis.

All the wonderful stories I could tell you about Marlene are not for LIFE. She would not mind and I would not mind. But many people would. Marlene makes her own rules in this life but the standards of conduct and of decency in human relationships that she imposes on herself are no less strict than the original ten.

That is probably what makes her mysterious: that anyone so beautiful and talented and able to do what she wants should only do what she believes to be absolutely right and to have had the intelligence and the courage to make the rules she follows.

She loves writing and is an intelligent and scrupulous critic and the happiest time I have is when I have written something that I am sure is good and she reads it and likes it. Since she knows about the things I write about which are people, country, life and death and problems of honor and of conduct, I value her opinion more than that of many critics. Since she knows about love, and knows that it is a thing which exists or does not exist, I value her opinion there more than that of the professors. For I think she knows more about love than anyone.

My wife Mary admires Marlene and thinks she is one of the finest women in the world. She knows some fine and wonderful stories too. But she said she would rather put it that way.

I know that everytime I have seen Marlene Dietrich ever, it has done something to my heart and made me happy. If this makes her mysterious then it is a fine mystery. It is a mystery we have known about for a long time.

The five-million-copy run of the issue sold out within two days.

Comment on *The Old Man and the Sea*, *Life* 33 (25 August 1952): 124.

Hemingway's statement on his novelette was provided as a promotional piece for its pre-book publication in Life, *but it serves other purposes. It makes the correct claim that his Nobel Prize is overdue, and it conveys the fake simplicity that afflicted his literary expression after 1950. It is unlikely that Hemingway read* The Old Man and the Sea 200 *times; the rest of the final paragraph is embarrassing, as is the novelette. In book form it remained on the* New York Times *best-seller list for twenty-six weeks.*

"I'm very excited about *The Old Man and the Sea* and that it is coming out in LIFE so that many people will read it who could not afford to buy it. That makes me much happier than to have a Nobel Prize. To have you guys being so careful and good about it and so thoughtful is better than any kind of prize. . . .

"Whatever I learned is in the story but I hope it reads simply and straight and all the things that are in it do not show but only are with you after you have read it. . . .

"I had wanted to write it for more than 15 years and I never did it because I did not think I could. . . . Now I have to try to write something better. That is sort of rough. But I had good luck with this all the way and maybe I will have luck again. . . .

"Don't you think it is a strange damn story that it should affect all of us (me especially) the way it does? I have had to read it now over 200 times and everytime it does something to me. It's as though I had gotten finally what I had been working for all my life. . . ."

"A Letter from Ernest Hemingway" by Earl Wilson, *New York Post*, 31 August 1952, 8M.

Earl Wilson (1907–87) wrote a syndicated gossip column, in which he frequently mentioned Hemingway.

Ernest Hemingway has them all yakking about him again. Nobody in the writing racket keeps them yakking like he does.

This time it's good yakking, about his new book, "The Old Man and the Sea."

So I'm going to publish a recent letter he wrote me, before the book came out.

He typed it on July 11, probably at 6 or 7 a.m. That's about the time he starts work every day.

You see, I'd written to him, asking if he'd explain why he lives in Cuba. After all, the greatest American author living in Cuba . . .

* * *

Some people thought he felt "shackled," or something, here.

Not at all, as you'll see from this letter. It starts out with a reference to my campaign to abolish "very" and other "useless" words. Anyway:

"Finca Vigia, San Francisco de Paula, Cuba.

"Dear Earl: Thanks for the letter. What are you abolishing 'very' for, boy? I still have to use it.

"You say a man is tired. Later on you say 'He was very tired now.' What's wrong with that?

"You ask me about why I live in Cuba. You've been out at the place: Didn't it seem like a good place to work and live and keep in shape to write as well as I can?

"I always had good luck writing in Cuba. First I used to come over from Key West when there were too many people around and work at the Ambos Mundos Hotel.

"It is close to the water front and I would get up at daylight and work and then go out on the boat and fish.

"Later on I moved from Key West over here in 1938 and rented this farm and finally bought it when For Whom the Bell Tolls came out.

* * *

"It is a good place to work because it is out of town and on a hill so that it is cool at night.

"I wake up when the sun rises and go to work and when I finish I get a swim and have a drink and read the N. Y. and Miami papers.

"After work you can fish or go shooting and in the evening Mary and I read and listen to music and go to bed. Sometimes we go into town or go to a concert. Sometimes we go to a fight or see a picture and go to La Floridita afterwards.

"Winter we can go to the Jai Alai.

"Mary loves to garden and has a good flower and vegetable garden and fine roses.

"I miss going around the joints and seeing the boys but every once in a while we get to town and you know we have fun then.

"I lost about five years work out of my life during the war and I am trying to make up for it now.

"I can't work and hang around New York because I never learned how to do it.

"When I hit New York it is like somebody coming off a long cattle drive hitting Dodge City in the old days. Right now I'm driving cattle and it is a long tough drive.

*   *   *

"But this fall when The Old Man and the Sea comes out you'll see some of the result of the last five years' work.

"All my life I have worked in all kinds of different places.

"For Whom the Bell Tolls I wrote here on the farm outside of Havana and part of it at Sun Valley in the quiet time out there between the summer and the winter season.

"I remember I started A Farewell to Arms in Paris, worked on it here, in Key West, Kansas City and finished it in Sheridan and Big Horn, Wyoming.

"The Sun Also Rises I started in Valencia, Spain, worked on it in Madrid, then Hendaye, France, and finished the first draft in Paris. I rewrote it in Schruns, Austria, and did the proofs at Juan les Pins.

"The reason I work here is because I like it here and I love my life with Mary and the fun she has with this hilltop and because I work well here. Is that what you wanted to know?

"You find me a place in Ohio where I can live on the top of a hill and be 15 minutes away from the Gulf Stream and have my own fruit and vegetables the year around and raise and fight game chickens without breaking the law and I'll go live in Ohio if Miss Mary and my cats and dogs agree.

"Best to you, Rosemary and El Slugger.

"Yours always, Papa."

~

"A Letter from Hemingway," *Saturday Review* 35 (6 September 1952): 11.

[Saturday Review] EDITOR'S NOTE: Whenever possible, material for this column is obtained in interviews with the author of the cover book for the week. In this case, however, it was impossible, since Mr. Hemingway resides in a suburb of Havana. So, Bernard Kalb, our interviewer, wrote Mr. Hemingway on Aug. 15, though neither his publisher nor his agent would bet on a reply. He wrote that he had to do a "400-word-or-so talk with Hemingway," and that he'd been advised to look up old clippings. "There are about five or six inches of clips in all," the letter read, "the first of them dating back to January 1919. It's history and it's fine, but it would be a lot better if there was something fresher. From my reading of the clips, I got the distinct impression that a good deal of the mail you receive winds up in the sea. I hope this letter doesn't." It went on to ask "how the writing is going, how the big book is coming and when we may expect it, how the fish are biting," adding that there was "a crazy deadline to meet—next Wednesday, Aug. 20, or a day later at the latest." The following reply came by return mail.

August 17, 1952

Dear Mr. Kalb:

Your letter came this morning and today is Sunday. Your deadline is Wednesday. So this may be worthless to you.

Let's skip the clippings. There will be new ones now. Anyway, for better or for worse, you wouldn't want a man to believe his own clippings, would you? He would certainly get confused over a period of thirty-four years.

Four hundred words are a lot of words on a Sunday morning unless you are delivering the sermon. Maybe we better put this in question and answer form.

Question: How is the writing going?

Answer: About the same as always. Some days better than others. I've worked two and a half years steady now and could use a vacation.

Question: How is the big book?

Answer: Very long. I am in no hurry about it.

Question: When may we expect it?

Answer: As and when it seems best to publish it.

Question: Do you mean your answers to be curt?

Answer: No, truly. I do not like to talk about my work when I am writing it. Some people do. But, unfortunately, I don't.

Question: How is the fishing?

Answer: It was very good through Spring and early summer. It was worthless during the time of the sun spots and is picking up again now with a very heavy current in the Gulf Stream. We've caught twenty-five marlin this season and should get quite a few more. The best year I ever had we caught fifty-four. The fish that are running now are very big. I work in the early morning and fish when I've finished work.

These are all the questions you asked, Mr. Kalb, and we are pretty short on the four hundred words. Would it be any use to know that it has been pleasant and cool here at the farm all summer?

(We had our heat-wave last year.)

The other night it was so cool coming in from the Gulf Stream that I had to put on a flannel shirt and last night I put on a sweater steering home. Mary, my wife, is very well. She loves the ocean and has never been sea-sick and she fishes beautifully. She sleeps in the morning while I wake and work early and she handles all the problems, when she wakes, that I neglect because my head is in the writing. She reads what I write most days and I can tell if it moves her if it gives her gooseflesh. She can't simulate gooseflesh. Now I had better knock-off writing this and write something else.

Good luck.
Yours always,
Ernest Hemingway

"Books I Have Liked," *New York Herald Tribune Book Review,* 7 December 1952, 9.

Hemingway's selection of Lillian Ross's book about the making of the Red Badge of Courage *movie may have been meant to show that her destructive 1950* New Yorker *profile hadn't damaged him. The recommendation of Edmund Wilson's collection of essays about the Twenties put an end to a feud with the critic that resulted from Wilson's "Ernest Hemingway: Bourdon Gauge of Morale" (Atlantic 164 [July 1939]: 36–46) and collected in* The Wound and the Bow *(New York: Oxford University Press, 1941).*

ERNEST HEMINGWAY: *Picture,* by Lillian Ross; *Rumor and Reflection,* by Bernard Berenson; *The Shores of Light,* by Edmund Wilson.

Endorsement, *Cuba: Isla de las Maravillas* by Ernesto T. Brivio (Havana: Empressa Editora de Publicaciones, 1953), 1.

The statement in Hemingway's hand appeared on the first page of this tourist guide.

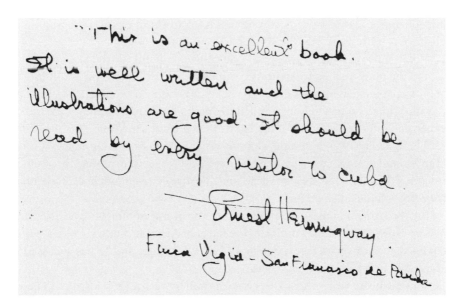

Location: Speiser and Easterling-Hallman Foundation Collection of Ernest Hemingway, Thomas Cooper Library, University of South Carolina.

Foreword, *Man and Beast in Africa* by François Sommer, translated by
Edward Fitzgerald (London: Jenkins, [1953]; New York: Citadel, 1954).
Location of Citadel edition: Speiser and Easterling-Hallman Foundation
Collection of Ernest Hemingway, Thomas Cooper Library, University of
South Carolina. Originally published as *Pourquoi ces Bêtes Sont-Elles
Sauvages,* with Hemingway's preface translated into French by Paule de
Beaumont (Paris: Nouvelles Éditions de la Toison D'or, 1951). Location:
Collection of Matthew J. and Arlyn Bruccoli.

*Sommer (1904–73) was a French photographer and big-game hunter. In this
foreword Hemingway out-experts the expert author. He also provides an egregious example of his corny nature communion: "At forty-five [fifty-four in
1953], having killed many, you would not kill a bear under any circumstances
because you have learned, over the years, that he is your brother."*

This is an excellent, well-informed and well-lived book on shooting game
animals in Africa. The historical research and the technical information is
sound and it shows the hunter as a man of delicacy and good will toward animals. This is a quality that only hunters will appreciate or know to be possible.
It is written for hunters. But it is also written for anyone who cares for Africa.
The book needs no preface any more than François Sommer would need an
introduction in any part of Africa he might go to shoot or to photograph in.
His face is more valid than most people's passports.

What is there, then, to say? First one can be grateful for the late information in the book written by someone who is truly trustworthy. I was disgusted
and disappointed at some of the things he wrote about current practices among
certain White Hunters in Kenya and Tanganyika but I suppose they were to be
expected with the evolution of the Safari into a conducted tour.

There always was a certain amount of shady work among some White
Hunters and at least two of my own fellow countrymen were among those who
offended the most. But they are dead and, fittingly enough, their deaths came
from the animals themselves.

But François Sommer has avoided bitterness and arguments and tried to
make a true picture of the hunting in the parts of Africa he knows. He has written vivid accounts with true modesty and excellent taste and he has succeeded
admirably in what he set out to do.

This begins to read more like a citation than a preface. In a way it is. There
are few things more difficult to write than stories of hunting without having
them turn into tales of butchery. Certainly one must butcher after the hunt. But
that is not what the hunt is about.

If a hunter writes of the chase and it becomes obvious that he loves the animals he hunts it is very easy to brand him as hypocritical or false. While actually he is simply human with his good parts and his deep and ancient faults. He is as Mr. Sommer says, "Not an angel."

It would be a strange thing if people with hunting in their blood for many hundreds of years would suddenly be without that taste. But it is a taste, and a hunger, too, that can be satisfied or partially satisfied.

In each person the changes come in a different way. There is no sudden thing such as happened to Saint Paul or to Saint Ignatius Loyola for any who tries to kill cleanly and never to excess.

At seventeen you would rather kill a grizzly bear than any other thing. At forty-five, having killed many, you would not kill a bear under any circumstances because you have learned, over the years, that he is your brother. But you would kill a *sanglier*. You are not yet ready to be brothers with the *sanglier* and you will still kill your pheasants high and clean as long as you have eyes to do so. Then what? Then you will try to get better shooting glasses.

The good hunter and the good amateur photographer never look for thrills nor for dangerous situations. They know these will come soon enough without looking for them. It is that basic knowledge that gives Mr. Sommer's book such a sound and healthy quality. It is that and his complete lack of chauvinism that makes him able to write of the good and bad aspects of shooting in the French possessions in Africa and in British East Africa. He does not write with detachment but rather with a sane and comprehensive love for the two very different places and the sound understanding and forgiving of faults which comes only with knowledge and long, unbigoted experience.

If I may add one technical observation it is this: a very strong case can be made for using only solids on all African game. You can then take a shot from any angle if you know anatomy and the solid bullet will not break up, nor expand and slow up. It will continue straight on its course toward the vital organ you intend it to pierce. Shooting by anatomy from any angle with solids is the deadliest and most merciful way to hunt. But first the hunter must learn the anatomy of his animals properly. Then, until he is really "checked out" he should see each animal skinned and butchered and trace the paths and results of his shots. Eventually he will be like a surgeon except that he will be armed with the lightning rapier of the long-reaching solid instead of a scalpel. Then he should try to take his shots closer and closer: for the pleasure of the stalk and to be able to apply his surgery the better.

The other practical thing I have found to be most useful in shooting all sorts of game is to have the trigger pull on all your rifles identical. Then you will not flinch nor hesitate on the different pulls but will squeeze them all the same whether it is the .256 Mannlicher or the .505 Gibbs. After a shooter has been punished badly by a big rifle, so that he has a bone-bruise for example, he will often flinch even on game. What he will do on a target, in error, with a big rifle must be seen to be believed. But with the same trigger pull as on his small rifle the shot comes clean before he has a chance to flinch against the imminent recoil.

These things are not necessary to the preface. But they might be of use. F. Sommer is absolutely sound in his basic feeling toward the different calibres for anyone making a short safari and the necessity for a knock-down weapon, especially to back up anyone who gets in trouble making photographs. In that case the trouble is already arrived and you need the whole Fire Department to put it out: and very quickly.

Now let us stop the preface and get to the book.

Hemingway during his 1935 safari. Location: Hemingway Collection, John F. Kennedy Library.

Preface, *Salt Water Fishing* by Van Campen Heilner, 2nd ed. rev. (New York: Knopf, 1953). Location: C. E. Frazer Clark Collection, University of Maryland Libraries.

Heilner (1899–1970) was an author, explorer, and sportsman.

It is good to have a book on Salt Water Fishing as a sport by Van Campen Heilner. He fished in the early days of big-game fishing on the Atlantic and Pacific Coasts and fished out of Bimini long before most of today's famous fishermen had ever heard the name of that place. He fished for sport rather than publicity, and he fished as inexpensively as possible.

Anyone with enough money and time, with modern tackle and equipment, good boats and expert guides, can catch huge fish if he wants to stay at it. All he needs is to go where they run, in the seasons that they run, and put in his time fishing and following his guides' instructions. Sooner or later, with a little luck, he will be a champion, especially if he tries for tuna. Marlin is considerably more difficult. Broadbill is more expensive as it takes more time and more money to get to where the biggest broadbill really are. And once there, a man would have to beat that great pioneer, George Tuker, which is difficult. Because Tuker happens to be a great fisherman and the broadbill run in his front yard.

But Salt Water Big Game Fishing, in some parts of the world, has degenerated into a sport where the man with the most money has far the best chance to catch the biggest fish, provided he puts in enough time at it. Consequently, at certain well known tournaments it has become a social sport, due to the costs of fishing, excluding better fishermen than those who become the champions.

Salt Water Fishing is a sport for everyone. All branches of it are fun. There is no game fish, from the gray snapper to the Mako shark, which does not give pleasure to the angler. The Mako gives him a little something else too. I only wish that the Mako, the blue-fin tuna, the big marlin and the broadbill were within reach of all anglers.

Van Heilner was a pioneer in Salt Water Fishing. He found out quite early that he had more fun with the bonefish on the flats and the tarpon up the jungle rivers and with surf casting than with the huge fish for which no labor-saving tackle had yet been devised. But he kept up with the major developments in heavy game fishing and he has been a Vice-President of the International Game Fish Association since that organization was founded. The I.G.F.A. is under the American Museum of Natural History, with which Van has long been associated, and it authenticates all Big Game Fish records.

Van Campen Heilner is a fine sportsman and a beautiful duck-shot as well as an old-timer in fishing. He has much to teach and he is always learning. I do not know anything better to say about a fisherman.

Finca Vigia
San Francisco de Paula, Cuba
June 1951

❧

"The Circus," *Ringling Bros and Barnum & Bailey Circus Magazine & Program* (1953): 7, 62.

The circus is the only ageless delight that you can buy for money. Everything else is supposed to be bad for you. But the Circus is good for you. It is the only spectacle I know that, while you watch it, gives the quality of a truly happy dream. The big cats do things no cat would ever do. You can see them jumping effortlessly over Mr. Konyct's head instead of making that unbelievable low rush they close with in the dusk when the female lion shows her cubs the way to kill.

The Circus bulls are disciplined and can make you feel that they are gay. They do not spread their ears and raise their trunks and come crashing through the bush.

The bears ride bicycles and dance and they would all get drunk if the Klausser family let them. You have known grizzlies to do very different things. But it was always because men intruded on their natural lives.

But in the Circus it is like a dream. The animals are dream animals. The riders are dream riders. The flyers really fly and catch each other the way you are caught in good dreams.

The horses make the loveliest pattern of dreams and the best are the free horses. You get from the clowns just what you bring to them. As well as that which shows, they bring a great baggage of old mockeries and deflations that are as old as our conceits and self-delusions. They also bring the true comic that makes the dreams we wake from laughing.

You watch Jeannie do everything gracefully and beautifully with her great versatility and you think what sort of a short-stop she would have been if she had been born a boy. If she had not been able to hit any better than Durocher, even, she could have stayed in the Big Leagues forever. In your dreams you watch Unus standing on one finger and you think, "Look at such a fine, intelligent and excellent man making his living standing on one finger when most of us can't even stand on our feet."

It isn't all just a lovely dream though. With some of the people you sweat their acts out with them the way they sweat them out themselves. Some of the people you do not like. But you find that you are in pretty good company. Hardly anybody else likes them either. Maybe their mothers do. Try to pick them out. There have to be a few villains in the best of dreams in order that there be Giants for Jack and Goliaths for Young David with the sling and the pebble. There has to be a dragon for St. George to kill. Or how would he get to be St. George and you get to be you and I get to be me? Pick out a couple of villains and hate them hard. But never hate any body when they are up there on the high wire; nor if they do triple somersaults; nor if they work with cats; nor bears with the muzzles off; nor if they do not make much money.

After you go home, having seen the show and now owning it so that it is part of your experience, remember the thousands and thousands of hours that went into making its beautiful precision and perfection. Stand on your finger a little bit like Unus. Make your motor-cycle lie down in the back yard and put a candle on one of the pedals and practice cutting the wick off the way Mroczkowski does with that palomino.

It is easy to rig a slack wire and you can get to be pretty good at it. Make a little bit like Dieter Tasso. In your dreams maybe. It is all wonderfully easy in your dreams. That is the pay-off. Then figure out how to take the Big Top down, put it up, and feed the show, keep the animals healthy, keep the performers happy, pay everybody, keep John Ringling North happy (consult me on this), keep Henry Ringling North happy (I haven't been able to find him for years myself) and I think you can work gradually into a pretty good job. But you will have to try to beat this year's Circus and that will be difficult. I think it is the best that I have ever seen.

Location: Speiser and Easterling-Hallman Foundation Collection of Ernest
Hemingway, Thomas Cooper Library, University of South Carolina.

"Hemingway Pays His Respects to Oak Park Library," *Library Journal* 79
(15 February 1954): 292.

[*Library Journal* editorial note] During the year 1953 the Oak Park, Illinois,
Public Library celebrated its 50th Anniversary. Among the highlights of the
anniversary year was a letter from a native son of Oak Park and a frequent
user in times past of the Oak Park Public Library, the noted American novelist, Ernest Hemingway. In response to an invitation to send a message to the
library at the time of the 50th Anniversary dinner, from Cuba Mr. Hemingway wrote Frederick Wezeman, Chief Librarian, the following letter. The
Scoville Institute referred to in Hemingway's letter was the predecessor of the
public library and was founded in 1886.

Dear Mr. Wezeman:

   Thank you very much for your letter. Unfortunately I was at sea when the
anniversary dinner of the Library occurred or I would have sent you a message
telling you how much I owe to the Library and how much it has meant to me
all my life.

   If it is not too late could you see that this letter reaches those who were
present at the dinner? I would be very glad to pay for the cost of having it
mimeographed and, in any event, enclose a small check.

   If you find that I owe any fines or dues you can apply it against them.

   I was born thirteen years after Scoville Institute was founded so I cannot
really rate as an Old Timer. But I was frequenting the Library within 3 years
after the founding.

   If you would like to have a set of the books which Scribner's are publishing of mine for the Library I would be very happy to write in them if they
would be of any value or use to you.

   With sincere best wishes,

   (Signed) Ernest Hemingway

Enclosed Check $100.00

"So That a Brave Man's Story Can Be Told," *Life* 36 (7 June 1954): 25.

War photographer Robert Capa (1913–54), Hemingway's longtime friend, was killed on assignment in Indochina. The Life *obituary included this cabled statement from Hemingway.*

"He was a good friend and a great and very brave photographer. It is bad luck for everybody that the percentages caught up with him. . . . He was so much alive that it is a hard long day to think of him as dead."

Nobel Prize Acceptance Statement, Read by John C. Cabot, U.S. Ambassador to Sweden, 10 December 1954. Reprinted fom *Conversations with Ernest Hemingway,* **ed. Matthew J. Bruccoli (Jackson: University Press of Mississippi, 1986), 196.**

Hemingway's illness following the African plane crashes prevented him from attending the Nobel Prize ceremony. The opening sentence refers to Faulkner's grandiloquent acceptance speech in 1949.

Having no facility for speech-making and no command of oratory nor any domination of rhetoric, I wish to thank the administrators of the generosity of Alfred Nobel for this Prize.

No writer who knows the great writers who did not receive the prize can accept it other than with humility. There is no need to list these writers. Everyone here may make his own list according to his knowledge and his conscience.

It would be impossible for me to ask the Ambassador of my country to read a speech in which a writer said all of the things which are in his heart. Things may not be immediately discernible in what a man writes, and in this sometimes he is fortunate; but eventually they are quite clear and by these and the degree of alchemy that he possesses he will endure or be forgotten.

Writing, at its best, is a lonely life. Organizations for writers palliate the writer's loneliness but I doubt if they improve his writing. He grows in public stature as he sheds his loneliness and often his work deteriorates. For he does his work alone and if he is a good enough writer he must face eternity, or the lack of it, each day.

For a true writer each book should be a new beginning where he tries again for something that is beyond attainment. He should always try for something that has never been done or that others have tried and failed. Then sometimes, with great luck, he will succeed.

How simple the writing of literature would be if it were only necessary to write in another way what has been well written. It is because we have had such great writers in the past that a writer is driven far out past where he can go, out to where no one can help him.

I have spoken too long for a writer. A writer should write what he has to say and not speak it. Again I thank you.

The Nobel Prize medal was presented to Hemingway by Carl Borgenstierna, the Swedish ambassador to Cuba. Location: Hemingway Collection, John F. Kennedy Library.

Page from an early draft of Hemingway's Nobel Prize speech.
Location: Rare Books Division, New York Public Library.

◇

Blurb on back dust jacket of *Moon over Miami* by Jack Kofoed (New York: Random House, 1955). Location: Collection of Matthew J. and Arlyn Bruccoli.

Kofoed (1894–1979) was a Miami Herald *columnist for forty-four years.*

I have read Jack Kofoed with enjoyment for over twenty years . . . or whenever it was he started in New York.

Tribute to Ezra Pound, *Ezra Pound at Seventy* (Norfolk, Conn.: New Directions, 1955), 4. Location: Collection of Matthew J. and Arlyn Bruccoli.

Pound, who had broadcast propaganda messages for Mussolini during World War II, was found incompetent to stand trial for treason in 1946. He was committed to St. Elizabeths Hospital for the insane in Washington, D.C. Hemingway joined with Archibald MacLeish, Robert Frost, T. S. Eliot, and other writers to work for Pound's release and for the dismissal of the charges against him. Pound was released in April 1958.

ernest hemingway

Will gladly pay tribute to Ezra but what I would like to do is get him the hell out of St. Elizabeth's; have him given a passport and allow him to return to Italy where he is justly valued as a poet. I believe he made bad mistakes in the war in continuing to broadcast for that sod Mussolini after we were fighting him. But I also believe he has paid for them in full and his continued confinement is a cruel and unusual punishment.

~

Endorsement for Pan American Airlines, *Holiday* 19 (February 1956): 60. (overleaf)

Location: Matthew J. and Arlyn Bruccoli Collection of F. Scott Fitzgerald, Thomas Cooper Library, University of South Carolina.

~

Letter to University of Glasgow Students, *Newsweek* 48 (29 October 1956): 57.

To students of Scotland's University of Glasgow who want to elect grizzled ERNEST (Papa) HEMINGWAY, 57, to the nonpaying, honorary job of university Lord Rector, the Nobel Prize-winning novelist wrote: "Since my past experience is limited to having refused to run for alderman in the nineteenth ward in Chicago . . . and to contributing to the election of a sheriff in a Florida city, I am unfamiliar with the legal dimensions of your campaign. . . . Recently my dear friend, Averell Harriman . . . was accused of having spent $2 million in his unsuccessful campaign for the Democratic nomination. This is the type of campaign . . . that your candidate deplores. We must have no slush fund. . . . " Students agreed: "No slush funds—even if we knew what it meant."

ERNEST HEMINGWAY *says:*

"Each generation of Americans

...Why? Because you'll see your ow

Signed at the Finca Vigia, Cuba. Dec. 1st. 1955

"Pan American and I are old friends"

"We started flying commercially about the same time. They did the flying and I was the passenger. It turned out to be a good partnership.

"After the old Key West-Miami-Havana-Bahamas early days, there was the Pacific when you took a day to Midway—another to Wake—one more to Guam—one to Manila—then Hongkong.

"Flying in China you had to sweat out many things. But you never worried about equipment, maintenance nor any Pan American pilot. I feel as safe with Pan American as I do any morning I wake up to a good working day."

Only Pan American offers <u>overnight</u> service fro

New York, Boston, Philadelphia, Detroit, and Cl

to 25 European cities...Fly Now—Pay Later!

eds to re-discover Europe

ntry's destiny more clearly if you spend your next vacation abroad"

The Romans tried, but couldn't bridge the mighty floods of the Rhône River at Avignon. Here in the South of France, in the year 1177, Saint Benezeg built the famous stone bridge which lasted until 1680. Today, in a morning's drive from the Pan American airport at Nice, you can be dancing before lunch on the bridge where seven generations of Americans have sung: *"On y danse, tout en ronde."*

PAN AMERICAN
WORLD'S MOST EXPERIENCED AIRLINE

Quotation from *Time,* 29 October 1956, 47, on back dust jacket of *The Restlessness of Shanti Andía and Other Writings* by Pío Baroja, translated by Anthony Kerrigan (Ann Arbor: University of Michigan Press, 1959).

Hemingway had visited the dying Spanish writer Baroja (1872–1956), a visit that Time *reported.*

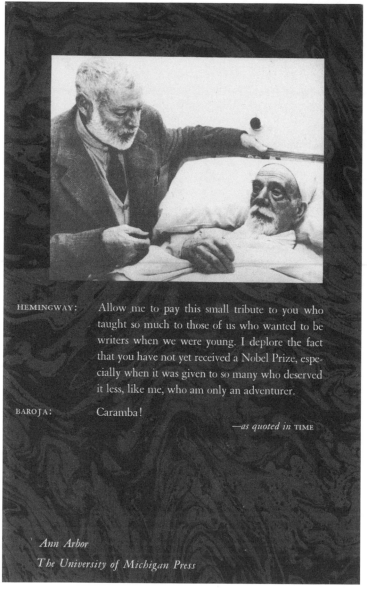

HEMINGWAY: Allow me to pay this small tribute to you who taught so much to those of us who wanted to be writers when we were young. I deplore the fact that you have not yet received a Nobel Prize, especially when it was given to so many who deserved it less, like me, who am only an adventurer.

BAROJA: Caramba!

—*as quoted in* TIME

Ann Arbor
The University of Michigan Press

Location: Collection of Matthew J. and Arlyn Bruccoli.

Blurb on front cover of *The Enemy* by Wirt Williams (New York: New American Library, 1957).

Williams (1921–86) and Hemingway were not friends; Hemingway admired this novel about submarines in World War II.

Location: Collection of Matthew J. and Arlyn Bruccoli.

COMBAT ACTION IN THE NORTH ATLANTIC . . . "A FIRST-RATE NOVEL OF THE WAY IT REALLY WAS."
— ERNEST HEMINGWAY

THE ENEMY

BY WIRT WILLIAMS
AUTHOR OF THE TROJANS

Blurb on front cover of *The Unquiet Grave: A Word Cycle* by Palinurus [Cyril Connolly] (New York: Viking, 1957). Location: Collection of Matthew J. and Arlyn Bruccoli.

British literary critic Connolly (1903–74) included both In Our Time *and* The Sun Also Rises *in his* The Modern Movement: One Hundred Key Books from England, France and America, 1880–1950 *(London: Hamish Hamilton, 1966).*

It is a book which, no matter how many readers it will ever have, will never have enough.

Blurb on back dust jacket of *The Professional* by W. C. Heinz (New York: Harper, 1958). Location: Collection of Matthew J. and Arlyn Bruccoli.

Heinz (b. 1915) was a sportswriter before he wrote books. In a 16 April 1970 letter to Bruccoli, he provided an account of his connection with Hemingway.

I do not know for sure how Hemingway got a copy of the book and his praise, while enormously appreciated, was not solicited by me. He cabled the publisher from Cuba post-publication, so his words did not get on the jacket, although they are on the second edition I mentioned above.

During World War II I was a war correspondent for The New York Sun and Hemingway, as you know, was reporting for Collier's. While the Fourth Infantry Division was fighting in the Huertgen Forest, Hemingway stayed in a fieldstone house at the edge of the woods and for several days several other correspondents and I stayed there with him. I doubt that he remembered me from that time, however, for after he praised my book I wrote him a letter of thanks and stated that I had been in that house with him. His reply did not indicate that he recalled me, but said that even if I had saved his life in the Huertgen he could not have written what he had about my book if he had not believed it.

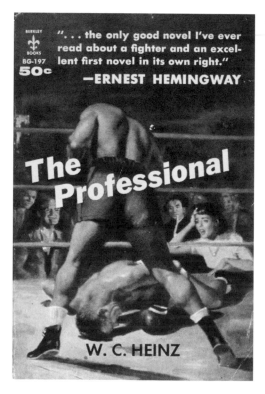

Hemingway's statement was also used on the 1959 Berkley paperback. Location: Collection of Matthew J. and Arlyn Bruccoli.

Foreword, *A Fly Fisher's Life* by Charles Ritz (New York: Holt, 1960).
Location: C. E. Frazer Clark Collection, University of Maryland Libraries.

Ritz (1892–1970) was the proprietor of the Ritz Hotel in Paris.

Charles Ritz is one of the very finest fishermen I know. He is not only a great fly fisherman for trout and salmon but he is an articulate writer and a splendid technician.

He is also an iconoclast who never hesitates to destroy an idol in order to deal only with true and important facts.

Because he is a charming companion he does not bore a non-technical reader with his knowledge. But it is there like a mine of true information for anyone with the desire and the intelligence to work it.

Fishing with Charles Ritz you come to know the streams of Normandy and Austria and the salmon rivers of the North.

As the world is run now few people can fish as far as Monsieur Charles fishes. No matter how it is run even fewer people could ever fish as well.

"Two Prideful Rivals and a Prideful 'Life,'" *Life* 41 (2 September 1960): 2.

Hemingway was unable to provide the five-thousand-word report of the Domínguín/Ordóñez competition that Life *had contracted for. The much-longer text was cut for him and published in three* Life *installments as "The Dangerous Summer." The introduction to the first installment quotes from a Hemingway letter to* Life *correspondent Will Lang.*

If I could have done it shorter I certainly would have. But it was necessary to make the people come alive and to show the extraordinary circumstances of what we both saw last summer and to make something which would have some unity and be worth publishing. Certainly the piece was worth more than the simple account of the mano a manos which were no longer news and had been picked over by various vultures and large-bellied crows. I now can write only one way: the best I can.

Statement on the 1961 Inauguration of President John F. Kennedy, *A Thou-sand Days* by Arthur M. Schlesinger Jr. (Boston: Houghton Mifflin, 1965), 732. Location: Special Collections, Thomas Cooper Library, University of South Carolina.

Because he was being treated for depression and hypertension at the Mayo Clinic, Hemingway was unable to accept an invitation to attend Kennedy's inaugural ceremonies. He sent this message to the president after watching the inauguration on television. In February 1961, after he had returned to Ketchum, Hemingway was invited to contribute a statement to a volume being presented to the president. He could not write even a few lines. After Heming-way's suicide five months later, Kennedy called him one of America's greatest authors and "one of the great citizens of the world."

Watching the inauguration from Rochester there was happiness and the hope and the pride and how beautiful we thought Mrs. Kennedy was. Watch-ing on the screen I was sure our President would stand any of the heat to come as he had taken the cold of that day. Each day since I have renewed my faith and tried to understand the practical difficulties of governing he must face as they arrive and admire the true courage he brings to them. It is a good thing to have a brave man as our President in times as tough as these are for our country and the world.

Blurbs on front and back dust jacket of *Out of My League* by George Plimpton (New York: Harper, 1961).

After Plimpton (1927–2003) interviewed Hemingway for the Paris Review *in 1951, they developed a warm friendship.*

"Beautifully observed and incredibly conceived, this account of a self-imposed ordeal has the chilling quality of a true nightmare. It is the dark side of the moon of Walter Mitty." —ERNEST HEMINGWAY

OUT OF MY LEAGUE

A weekend athlete and full-time man-of-letters recalls his eye-opening and very funny experience pitching against the greatest pros in baseball.

GEORGE PLIMPTON

Location: Matthew J. and Arlyn Bruccoli Collection of George Plimpton, Thomas Cooper Library, University of South Carolina.

On back jacket: "'After reading *Out of My League* it is very hard to wait for the true story of George and Archie Moore.'—Ernest Hemingway"

Blurb on front flap of *To the Bullfight Again: A Spectator's Guide* by John Marks, enlarged and rev. ed. (New York: Knopf, 1967). Location: Collection of Matthew J. and Arlyn Bruccoli.

John H. P. Marks (b. 1908) was a bullfight aficionado, a translator of French and Spanish authors, and a journalist for the London Times *and the BBC.*

"The best book on the subject—after mine," Ernest Hemingway assured the author of *To the Bullfight* (1953) in Pamplona when he, "Papa"—beaming, grizzled—returned with nostalgia to Spain, the wars over. He confirmed this handsome compliment later to a mutual friend, but phrased it still more generously, saying "by a foreigner" instead of "after mine."

Further Reading

Baker, Carlos. *Ernest Hemingway: A Life Story*. New York: Scribners, 1969. Standard one-volume biography.

———. *Supplement to Ernest Hemingway: A Comprehensive Bibliography*. Princeton: Princeton University Press, 1975. Primary and secondary.

———, ed. *Ernest Hemingway: Selected Letters, 1917–1961*. New York: Scribners, 1981.

Bruccoli, Matthew J., ed. *Conversations with Ernest Hemingway*. Jackson: University Press of Mississippi, 1986. Interviews.

———, ed., with Judith S. Baughman. *The Sons of Maxwell Perkins: Letters of F. Scott Fitzgerald, Ernest Hemingway, Thomas Wolfe, and Their Editor*. Columbia: University of South Carolina Press, 2004.

———, ed., with the assistance of Robert W. Trogdon. *The Only Thing That Counts: The Ernest Hemingway/Maxwell Perkins Correspondence 1925–1947*. New York: Scribner, 1996.

Hanneman, Audre. *Ernest Hemingway: A Comprehensive Bibliography*. Princeton: Princeton University Press, 1975. Primary and secondary.

Raeburn, John. *Fame Became of Him: Hemingway as Public Writer*. Bloomington: Indiana University Press, 1984. Critical study.

Reynolds, Michael. *The Young Hemingway*. New York: Basil Blackwell, 1986.

———. *Hemingway: The Paris Years*. New York: Basil Blackwell, 1989.

———. *Hemingway: An Annotated Chronology*. Detroit: Manly/Omnigraphics, 1991.

———. *Hemingway: The American Homecoming*. Cambridge, Mass.: Blackwell, 1992.

———. *Hemingway: The 1930s*. New York: W. W. Norton, 1997.

———. *Hemingway: The Final Years*. New York: W. W. Norton, 1999. Standard multivolume biography.

Sandison, David. *Ernest Hemingway: An Illustrated Biography*. Chicago: Chicago Review Press, 1999. Pictorial biography.

Stephens, Robert O. *Hemingway's Nonfiction: The Public Voice*. Chapel Hill: University of North Carolina Press, 1968. Critical study.

Voss, Frederick, with an essay by Michael Reynolds. *Picturing Hemingway: A Writer in His Time*. Washington, D.C.: Smithsonian National Portrait Gallery/New Haven and London: Yale University Press, 1999. Pictorial biography.